WILLIAM HOWARD TAFT
1857-1930

Chronology-Documents-Bibliographical Aids

Edited by
Gilbert J. Black

Series Editor
Howard F. Bremer

1970
OCEANA PUBLICATIONS, INC.
Dobbs Ferry, New York 10522

Library of Congress Catalog Card Number: 70-16059
International Standard Book Number: 0-379-12080-1

Manufactured in the United States of America

CONTENTS

EDITOR'S FOREWORD

Students of history, modern government or sociology should find this book useful for organizing and researching an important man and an important period in the recent past of our country. In the chronology we have attempted to present facts rather than opinion. Material has been chosen for its relevance to today's problems. The bibliography reflects material in print or generally available in libraries, with emphasis on paperback editions.

The editor wishes to acknowledge the immense help of his wife, Betty, without whom this book could not have been written. Both of us want to thank Mr. Richard Maass, whose extensive library and thorough knowledge of history were of great help, as well as the librarians at the White Plains, Scarsdale and New York City libraries. Documents in this volume are taken from James D. Richardson, editor, Messages and Papers of the Presidents. Vol. 16 & 17.

CHRONOLOGY
EARLY YEARS

1857

September 15:   Born: Cincinnati, Ohio. Father: Alphonso, an attorney; mother: Louise Torrey, his father's second wife. There were two surviving boys, Charles Phelps and Peter Rawson, from his father's first marriage to Fannie Phelps, who died in 1852.

1859

May 27   Brother, Henry Waters, born.

1861

December 28   Brother, Horace Dutton, born.

1863

Fall   Entered Sixteenth District Public School in the Mt. Auburn section of Cincinnati, where the family home was located.

1865

July 18   Sister, Frances Louise, born.

December   Father accepted an interim appointment as judge of the Cincinnati Supreme Court. Four years later he was nominated for the post by both the Republicans and the Democrats.

1866

June 6   Suffered a slight fracture and a bad cut on the head when the horses drawing the family carriage ran off.

1869

December 24   In a letter to Taft's aunt, Delia Torrey, his father reported that Taft was first in his class with an average of 95.

1

1874

June

Graduated from Woodward High School in downtown Cincinnati as salutatorian.

August 12

Judge Alphonso Taft, his father, was principal speaker at a reunion of almost 1000 members of the Taft family at Uxbridge, Massachusetts.

September

Entered Yale University.

1876

Father served as Secretary of War and attorney general under President U.S. Grant.

1878

June 25

Delivered senior oration in which he talked about political corruption, the importance of an educated citizenry and the waning popularity of the Republican Party.

June 27

Graduated from Yale second in a class of 132.

Summer

Started reading law in his father's office.

Fall

Entered Cincinnati Law School and worked part time as a reporter for the Cincinnati Commercial covering the courts.

1879

Father was defeated for the Republican nomination for Governor of Ohio.

CAREER
1880

Summer

Graduated from law school and admitted to the Ohio bar; however continued working as a reporter rather than enter private practice.

October 25

Appointed assistant prosecutor of Hamilton County, at a salary of $1,200 per year, to begin January 3, 1881.

Fall	Campaigned throughout the state for the Republican state and national ticket.

1882

January	Appointed United States collector of internal revenue for the first district of Ohio by President Arthur.
April 17	Former Congressman Thomas L. Young wrote Taft ask ing him to fire several men in the internal revenue de- partment whom he said were against his renomination. Taft felt that these particular men were "perhaps the best men in the service" and refused to discharge them. As a result he was criticized for disloyalty to the party. Father appointed minister to Austria by President Arthur.
December	Announced his resignation as collector which became effective March, 1883. He then formed a law partner- ship with Major Harlan Page Lloyd, a former associate of his father.

1883

Summer	Visited his parents at the American embassy in Vienna. Also saw Ireland, Scotland and England and went on hik- ing trip in Switzerland with boyhood friend, Rufus Smith.
October	Returned home and campaigned for Joseph B. Foraker, the Republican candidate for governor. Democrat, George Hoadley, one of Taft's former law school pro- fessors, was elected.

1884

Fall	President Arthur was his choice for the Republican nom- ination, but when James G. Blaine won, Taft campaigned for him. Father appointed United States minister to Russia.

1885

January 1   Appointed assistant county solicitor. (Rufus Smith, his close friend, was county solicitor.) The salary from his post, $2,500, plus the income from his private practice brought his earnings for 1885 to $5,000.

January 5   Delivered the summation in the disbarment trial of Thomas C. Campbell, a noted Cincinnati criminal lawyer, who had been successful in defending many controversial clients. On February 3, the court exonerated Campbell except for one minor charge.

November   Joseph B. Foraker was elected governor of Ohio.

1886

June 19   Married Helen (Nellie) Herron, daughter of a Cincinnati attorney. After a wedding trip through France, England and Scotland, they returned in the fall to their new house in the Walnut Hills section of Cincinnati.

1887

March   Appointed judge of the Superior Court by Governor Foraker to fill the vacancy created by the resignation of Judge Judson Harmon.

1888

April   Elected to full term as Superior Court judge. Two noted jurists were his colleagues, Judges Hiram Peck and Frederick Moore. Later Judge Edward Noyes replaced Peck.

1889

September 8   Son, Robert Alphonso, born.

September 18   Chided his brother Charles, who now owned a large interest in the Cincinnati Times-Star and was considering an independent political policy for the paper, "No matter how bad the Republican legislature ticket, the Democratic members will work more mischief."

1890

January

Wrote the opinion of the court in the decision against a bricklayer's union ruling that the secondary boycott was illegal. This decision was to hinder him when he campaigned for the Republican presidential nomination.

February 14

Sworn in as solicitor general of the United States. Governor Foraker, Judge Peck and other jurists had suggested Taft for the existing vacancy on the United States Supreme Court, which was already and would remain the main ambition of his life.

March

The Tafts rented a small house at 5 DuPont Circle in Washington, D.C., for $100 a month. Taft's only income was the $7,000 a year salary of solicitor general.

1891

February

Fearing that unrestricted fishing was exterminating the herds of seal in the Bering Sea, the United States seized sealing vessels. England appealed to the United States Supreme Court to prohibit the sale of a confiscated Canadian ship. In a case that drew much public attention, Taft, as solicitor general, argued before the court that when diplomatic negotiations were in progress, a foreign power could not ask for a review of conduct before another branch of the government. The court concurred and refused to enjoin the sale.

May 21

Taft was with his father when he died in San Diego, California. His father had been sent to the drier climate for his health.

August 1

Daughter, Helen Herron, born.

1892

March 21

Resigned as solicitor general to become United States circuit judge for the Sixth Judicial Court and an ex-officio member of the Circuit Court of Appeals of the Sixth Circuit. The circuit included Ohio, Kentucky,

Michigan and Tennessee, required much travel and paid $6,000 a year. The family returned to Cincinnati. Since their house was leased to tenants, they moved to a rented house at Third and Lawrence Streets.

1893

April 3   Upheld an injunction, granted in the federal court, forcing various railroads to handle the freight of the Toledo, Ann Arbor and North Michigan Railway Company. This was, in effect, a decision against the Brotherhood of Locomotive Engineers, who were invoking By-Law No. 12, that stated that locomotive engineers could not handle property belonging to a struck railroad. This decision was also used against Taft by organized labor in the campaign of 1908.

1894

July 13   Sentenced Frank M. Phelan, an aide of Eugene Debs, to six months in Warren County jail for contempt for carrying out a boycott on all railroads running into Cincinnati which used Pullman cars. Taft's decision included the first clear judicial definition of the right to strike.

November   His brother, Charles, was elected to Congress.

1896

Became dean and professor of property at Cincinnati Law School. He taught two classes for two hours a week.

1897

September 20   Second son, Charles Phelps II, was born.

1898

February 8   Revived the Sherman Antitrust Act by handing down a decision that the Addystone Pipe and Steel Company of Cincinnati was guilty of combining to restrain interstate commerce.

1899

January 14   Informed in a letter from his brother, Henry, that there
                  was a movement at Yale supporting him for the presi-
                  dency of the university, he replied that he would not ac-
                  cept because of "two insuperable objections," his reli-
                  gion (Unitarianism) and his qualifications as an educator.

                  Found the Cleveland, Cincinnati, Chicago and St. Louis
                  Railway Company liable for a brakeman's injury due to
                  a safety violation that the brakeman had been aware of.
                  This was a reversal of past decisions of the Ohio Su-
                  preme Court and eventually ended the doctrine of as-
                  sumed risk as protection for employers.

1900

January   Summoned to Washington by President McKinley and of-
                  fered a place on the governing commission for the new-
                  ly-acquired Philippine Islands. Taft hesitated leaving
                  the judiciary but, mainly due to the persuasiveness of
                  Secretary of War, Elihu Root, he accepted under the
                  condition that he could head the commission.

April 17   Sailed from San Francisco for the Philippines with the
                  other members of the commission: General Luke E.
                  Wright, a Tennessee lawyer; Henry C. Ide, a New Eng-
                  land lawyer and former chief justice of Samoa; Dean C.
                  Worcester, a zoology professor from the University of
                  Michigan who had been a member of the first study com-
                  mission to the Philippines; and Bernard Moses, a history
                  professor from the University of California.

September 1   The document instructing the commission on the policy
                  to be followed in the Philippines became effective. It
                  was mainly the work of Taft and Secretary of War Root
                  and gave the civilian commission all legislative powers,
                  but the military governor remained the chief executive.
                  Taft soon felt this was the one flaw in the plan.

1901

March 22   Emilio Aguinaldo, the last of the insurgent generals at large was captured and on April 19, he took the oath of allegiance to the United States. In order to encourage other insurrectionists to surrender, the commission decreed that property and funds of all insurgents still in arms after April 1, 1901, would be confiscated and anyone still fighting on April 1, 1901, would be disenfranchised and ineligible for political appointments.

March 10   The commission, with wives and children, prominent Filipinos and newspapermen, embarked on a two-month tour of the southern provinces.

July 4   Taft took the oath as civil governor of the Philippines. Major General A. R. Chaffee replaced General MacArthur as military governor which was now the subordinate position. Taft named Commissioner Wright, Secretary of Commerce and Police; Ide, Secretary of Finance and Justice; Moses, Secretary of Public Instruction; Worcester, Secretary of Interior; three Filipinos were added to the commission.

September 14   Received word of President McKinley's death and wondered at the effect it would have on the Philippine program which the late President had strongly supported. Roosevelt had been Taft's choice for the 1904 presidential nomination, however, so Roosevelt had his complete support.

December 24   Returned to the United States with his family to recuperate from an operation, and also to be present in Washington for a series of Senate committee hearings on the Philippines.

1902

June 5   In an audience with Pope Leo XIII, Taft, as a special emissary of President Roosevelt, requested that the Spanish friars in the Philippines be replaced by another order and that their land be sold to the Philippine government at a fair price.

June 21   The Church agreed to sell the lands but would not promise to withdraw the friars. Root ordered Taft to end the negotiations. Taft felt it was important that the friars be replaced, as their political policies and unfair land leasing practices led to unrest and fighting. (The question was not to be settled until 1903 when at Taft's urging 390,000 acres of the friars' land was bought for $7,543,000. The land, in turn, was sold in small parcels on easy terms to the natives. Gradually, American and Filipino priests replaced the friars so that their importance dwindled and they no longer held political power.)

August 22   Arrived in Manila where the islands were just recovering from a cholera epidemic. In his speech to the crowd gathered to welcome him, he told of acts passed in Congress: the tariff to admit Philippine products to the United States at a rate 25% lower than other countries, the exclusion of Chinese labor, and the Philippines Government Bill, which gave extra powers to the local government and provided that within two years after a census had been taken a popular assembly would be created.

October 27   Taft declined an appointment to the Supreme Court proffered by President Roosevelt, because he felt it his duty to remain in the Philippines until it was over its economic crisis.

                                    1903

January 8   Again after a second request from the President to accept a Supreme Court seat, Taft cabled an appeal to remain in the Philippines.

December 23   Left Manila for Washington to replace Elihu Root as Secretary of War. His health (he had contracted amoebic dysentery) and the fact that the Philippines were

administered by the War Department in Washington
were two deciding factors in his acceptance of the post.
He was concerned about supporting his family and en-
tertaining in Washington on the cabinet salary of $8,000.
His brother, Charles, promised $6,000 annually, if
necessary.

1904

January 6   On trip home, lunched with the Emperor of Japan in
                 Tokyo.

February 1   Officially appointed Secretary of War by President Roo-
                 sevelt.

March 22   President Roosevelt announced to the Isthmian Canal
                 Commission that Secretary of War Taft would be in
                 general command. Rear Admiral John G. Walker, re-
                 tired, was first chairman.

Spring and   Taft went on the stump campaigning for Roosevelt's
Summer   election.

November 8   Roosevelt won election handily over his Democratic
                 opponent, Judge Alton Parker. Taft was already being
                 mentioned as the likely candidate for 1908, but he still
                 hoped for appointment as Chief Justice.

November 27   Arrived in the Panama Canal Zone on a good-will tour
                 to win the confidence of the Panamanians. Conferred
                 with John F. Wallace, the chief engineer of the project.
                 Taft was accompanied on the trip by William N. Crom-
                 well, the New York lawyer who had worked with Bunau-
                 Varilla and had earned $800,000 in legal fees for his
                 part in the canal deal.

1905

April 8   While Roosevelt vacationed in the Rockies, Taft was
                 left in charge of the difficult Dominican situation.

April 26   As acting Secretary of State, in John Hay's absence, Taft spoke to the British Ambassador, Sir Mortimer Durand, regarding the agreement on Morocco between France and England. The situation culminated in the Algeciras conference, where the United States sided with France and England against Germany.

June 28   John F. Stevens, a well-known railroad construction engineer, was chosen to replace Wallace as chief engineer of the Panama Canal.

July 27   In an interview with Count Taro Katsura, the Japanese premier, in Tokyo, Taft agreed that Japan should establish suzerainty over Korea.

Summer   Led a congressional junket to the Philippines in hope of influencing passage of measures to benefit the Philippines. Included in the group were President Roosevelt's daughter, Alice, and Representative Nicholas Longworth of Ohio, her future husband.

September   Began a diet under the care of a London doctor. By the summer of 1906 he was down from 320 to 250 pounds and felt much better.

October 21   In a campaign speech for the re-election of Governor Myron T. Herrick of Ohio, Taft repudiated Boss George B. Cox.

1906

April 18   Informed of the San Francisco earthquake, he immediately ordered army supplies and tents rushed to the disaster area.

August 14   A disorder in Brownsville, Texas, resulting in the death of at least one man was, after a brief investigation, blamed on members of three Negro companies. Roosevelt ordered a blanket discharge for the companies. Taft reluctantly signed the dismissal orders.

September 19   Taft and Acting Secretary of State Robert Bacon arrived in Havana, Cuba, on a fact-finding mission. A rebellion was in the making, threatening American military and business interests.

September 29   Appointed provisional governor of Cuba when Palma resigned and the United States intervened. Taft allowed Cuba's diplomatic functions to continue and demonstrated to the people that his position was only temporary until their government was once more stable.

October 13   Charles E. Magoon succeeded Taft as provisional governor of Cuba. On January 28, 1909, a new election was held under revised election laws. The Liberals won and the government was returned to Cuba.

October   Spoke in nine states for election of Republican congressmen. Roosevelt held that Taft was largely responsible for the Republican victory on election day.

December 12   William H. Moody was appointed to the seat on the Supreme Court that had been offered to Taft. Mrs. Taft and others had counseled Taft to decline because the 1908 presidential nomination would be his.

                            1907
February   John F. Stevens resigned as chief engineer and was replaced by Major George W. Goethals. Taft had met Goethals on his 1905 Panama trip and personally recommended him to Roosevelt.

April 30   In a speech in Madison Square Garden, William Jennings Bryan said that the railroads should become public property. This statement relieved Roosevelt, and hence Taft, of being placed in the position of radicals, and diminished Bryan's chances for election.

July 29   Senator Foraker announced against Taft's nomination for Presidency, but the Ohio Republican State Central Com-

mittee voted 15 to 6 in Taft's favor. This was the end
of Foraker's political power.

September 28   En route to the Philippines, Taft paid a return visit to
                Tokyo to reassure the Japanese of the United States'
                friendship. Taft reported to Roosevelt that the Japanese
                government was anxious to avoid war and was in no fi-
                nancial position to wage it.

October   Proceeded to Manila for the opening of the Assembly, the
                first step in self-government for the Philippines. On
                the trip home, he passed through Moscow and called on
                the Russian Czar.

December 7   Taft's mother died. Departing Hamburg the same day,
                Taft did not arrive in time for the funeral. His mother
                was one of the few who had advised him not to seek the
                Presidency.

                                   1908
April 1   Traveled as far west as Omaha in a final speaking tour
                before the Republican Convention.

May 17   Returned to Washington after a Panama trip made nec-
                essary by election troubles there.

June 18   Taft nominated for the presidency at the Republican Con-
                vention in Chicago. James S. Sherman (Sunny Jim) of
                New York was the vice-presidential nominee. Taft
                agreed to compromise wording of the injunction issue
                in the platform, which failed to satisfy both business
                and labor.

June 30   Resigned as Secretary of War to devote all his energies
                to the campaign.

July 8   Democratic Convention began in Denver. William Jen-
                nings Bryan won the Democratic presidential nomination.
                The platform did not mention government ownership of

railroads and, indeed, Bryan thought now that the answer might lie in stricter regulation.

September 17   Taft refused to answer Carry Nation's questions regarding his position on prohibition. He was in favor
of local option, believing a federal law would be unen-
forceable. His religion caused him problems during
the campaign; many voters writing to ask him if he rejected Christ. He was also highly criticized about his
favorite sport, golf.

September 19   Directed George R. Sheldon, treasurer of the Republican National Committee, not to accept any funds from
". . . the Standard Oil Company or anyone connected
with it." This was broadened further to include the
trusts and their people. It was deemed all right to accept $20,000 from Andrew Carnegie, as he had retired
from the steel industry.

November 3   Electoral vote was 321 for Taft to 162 for Bryan. Taft's
popular vote lead was less than half of Roosevelt's lead
in 1904.

December   Counseled by Roosevelt and Root, President-elect Taft
decided that he could not be successful in replacing
conservative Speaker of the House "Uncle Joe" Cannon.
This was a bitter blow to the insurgents, who had hoped
for Taft's support.

1909
February 1   Inspected work on the Panama Canal and was satisfied
with its progress.

TERM IN OFFICE

March 4   Due to inclement weather, Chief Justice Melville W.
Fuller administered the oath of office in the Senate
Chamber. Taft's cabinet was: Philander C. Knox,
Secretary of State; George W. Wickersham, Attorney

General; Jacob Dickinson, Secretary of War; Frank H. Hitchcock, Postmaster General; Charles Nagel, Secretary of Commerce and Labor; Richard A. Ballinger, Secretary of Interior; --all lawyers; Franklin MacVeagh, Secretary of Treasury; James Wilson, Secretary of Agriculture; and George von L. Meyer, Secretary of the Navy.

March — Congressional insurgents failed to unseat Speaker Cannon.

March 18 — Attended reunion at Yale where he was overwhelmingly greeted.

March 23 — Roosevelt left for African safari.

May 17 — Mrs. Taft suffered a stroke which left her with impaired speech.

June 16 — Recommended, in a message to Congress, a 2% tax on the net income of all corporations except banks, and adoption of a constitutional amendment permitting federal income taxes.

August 5 — Signed Payne-Aldrich Act, a compromise bill that was criticized for not lowering tariffs as extensively as many had hoped. The act created a Tariff Board to study the protective system and make recommendations.

September 17 — While on a 13,000-mile trip through the country, Taft defended the Payne-Aldrich Act. In a definitive speech at Winona, Minnesota, he said, "I think the Payne Bill the best bill that the Republican party ever passed." This sentence was headlined in the newspapers, causing unfavorable public reaction.

October 16 — Exchanged visits at El Paso, Texas, and Juarez, Mexico, with President Porfirio Diaz of Mexico, whose dictatorial power was being threatened.

November 10   Returned to Washington, having made 259 speeches.
                     The trip included steamboating down the Mississippi
                     where Taft pleaded for a comprehensive waterways and
                     conservation program rather than a pork barrel. Un-
                     wisely, as Archie Butt (White House aide) for one thought,
                     Taft was photographed with Speaker Cannon.

Fall   The Committee on Legislation of the American Bankers
                     Association warned against a central banking system,
                     and the radical ideas of Senator Aldrich's Monetary
                     Commission.

November 13   In an article in Collier's Weekly, Louis R. Glavis, chief
                     of the Field Division of the Interior Department, accused
                     Secretary of the Interior Ballinger of a conspiracy to
                     defraud the public domain in the Alaskan coal lands, and
                     the administration not taking action to prevent it. Taft,
                     after studying the facts, declared Ballinger innocent and
                     had Glavis fired.

November 20   The Standard Oil Company was found guilty of violating
                     the Sherman Law by being a monopoly. Frank B. Kel-
                     logg, later Secretary of State under Hoover, was the
                     special prosecutor for the government.

December 7   In his annual message, Taft pointed out that the $17,-
                     500,000 Post Office deficit was due in large part to low
                     postal rates for magazines and newspapers. This state-
                     ment angered many publishers who were instrumental
                     in forming public opinion for or against Taft, and was
                     an important factor in the 1910 congressional election.

December 20   Appointed Major General Leonard Wood, Roosevelt's
                     friend from before Rough Rider days, as Chief of Staff
                     to the United States Army.
                     Appointed Circuit Judge Horace H. Lurton, aged 69,
                     with whom he had served, Associate Justice of the Su-
                     preme Court to replace Rufus W. Peckham, over the
                     protests of Attorney General Wickersham (concerning

Lurton's age) and Gompers and other labor leaders (concerning his conservatism).

1910

January 7   Taft ordered Gifford Pinchot, a Roosevelt man, fired as chief of the United States Forest Service, when a letter was made public Pinchot had written to Senator Dolliver of Iowa appealing for two of his employees, who had been involved in the Glavis case.

February   Sent Secretary of State Knox on a fact-finding and good-will tour of Central and South America.

March 17   Representative George William Norris of Nebraska moved for the adoption of his resolution to elect the House Rules Committee instead of having the Speaker (Cannon, in this case) appoint them. After much debate, it was passed 191 to 156. A vote to unseat the Speaker was defeated, but his days of power were gone.

May 10   Requested Roosevelt to represent the United States as a Special Ambassador at the funeral of King Edward VII.

May 20   Congressional investigation cleared Secretary Ballinger and the Taft administration of land fraud. Attorney Louis D. Brandeis, who had been hired to represent Glavis at the hearings, brought to light the predating of a report made by Attorney General Wickersham. This threw new suspicion on the administration.

May 31   Obtained an injunction to prevent western railroads from raising freight rates in violation of the Sherman Act. On June 6, the railroads announced that they would delay raising the rates until new legislation was passed enabling the Interstate Commerce Commission to examine them.

June   Treasury Department began study of fiscal operations of government with a $100,000 allowance Congress appropriated at Taft's request.

June 18   Roosevelt returned from African and European tour to a tumultuous welcome. Taft sent his aide, Archie Butt, Secretary of Navy Meyer, and Secretary of Agriculture Wilson to represent him.

June 20   Roosevelt declined Taft's invitation to visit the White House.

June 25   Taft signed the Postal Savings Bank Act, establishing one bank in each state. It limited accounts to $500 giving two per cent interest and created a Board of Trustees composed of the Postmaster General, the Secretary of Treasury and the Attorney General, with wide discretionary powers. Deposits mainly were re-deposited in local banks.

June 30   Roosevelt, accompanied by Senator Henry Cabot Lodge, visited Taft at his summer quarters at Beverly, Massachusetts. No issues were discussed.

July 17   J. P. Morgan paid an unpublicized visit to Taft at the summer White House in Beverly. Taft had already angered the insurgents by playing golf with Henry C. Frick, whose summer place was nearby.

September 5   Taft rejected the suggestion that a dinner be given for him and Roosevelt at the National Conservation Congress at St. Paul. They spoke on different days instead.

September 10   Taft, in a letter to his brother after Roosevelt's Osawatomie "New Nationalism" speech, said that " . . . he (Roosevelt) has proposed a program which it is absolutely impossible to carry out except by a revision of the Federal Constitution."

September 19   Taft and Roosevelt, meeting at New Haven, Connecticut, discussed the New York State Republican Convention.

September 27   At Saratoga, Taft supported Roosevelt against Vice-
                president Sherman and the other Old Guard. Roose-
                velt's choice, Henry L. Stimson, won the nomination
                for governor.

October   Appointed Governor Charles Evans Hughes to be As-
                sociate Justice of the Supreme Court to replace David
                J. Brewer.

November 4   Democrats gained eight Senate seats and a majority of
                50 in the House. In New York, Stimson lost. Beveridge
                was defeated. Warren Harding, to whose campaign
                Taft had personally contributed $5,000, was defeated
                for Governor of Ohio. Woodrow Wilson was elected
                Governor of New Jersey.

November   Appointed Willis Van Devanter Associate Justice of the
                Supreme Court to replace William Moody, who resigned
                because of ill health.
                Left for an inspection trip of the Panama Canal. Re-
                turned just before Christmas.

December 6   In his Annual Message to Congress, Taft asked Con-
                gress to amend the injunction section of the antitrust
                law. Congress refused.
                Requested that Congress authorize a Tariff Commis-
                sion to replace the Tariff Board.

December 12   Associate Justice Edward D. White was elevated to
                Chief Justice of the Supreme Court to replace Fuller.
                Appointing White, a Democrat, Confederate veteran
                and a Roman Catholic, won almost unanimous approval
                from the bar.

December 24   Andrew Carnegie created the Carnegie Peace Fund with
                a donation of $10,000,000 and praised Taft's views of
                the necessity of arbitrating national honor, if neces-
                sary, to preserve peace.

1911

January

Appointed Joseph R. Lamar to be an Associate Justice of the Supreme Court.

February 15

United States Commerce Court opened as provided in an amendment to the Interstate Commerce Law, that also broadened the powers of the Interstate Commerce Commission.

March 2

Appointed a commission to investigate the postal rates for newspapers and magazines. The results of the study helped to convince Congress that a rate increase was justified.

March 6

American Ambassador to Mexico, Henry Lane Wilson, reported on the critical state of President Porfirio Diaz's government and on his concern for the safety of 40,000 American residents. Taft ordered the mobilization of 20,000 soldiers at the Mexican border, on the pretense of training maneuvers.

March 7

Appointed Walter L. Fisher, a conservationist and follower of Pinchot, Secretary of Interior to replace Richard Ballinger, who resigned.

March

Appointed Commission on Economy and Efficiency to study governmental organization.

May 16

Henry Stimson appointed Secretary of War to replace Dickinson.

May 24

President Diaz of Mexico resigned. Francisco Madero was elected President the following November, but unrest continued.

June 6

Treaty with Nicaragua signed, patterned after the Santo Domingo convention. The Senate failed to approve it.

June 17   Senator Robert LaFollette of Wisconsin announced his candidacy for Republican presidential nomination.

July 19   President and Mrs. Taft celebrated their silver wedding anniversary at the White House with a night garden party for 5,000 guests.

July 26   Signed Canadian Reciprocity Agreement for which he had made three trips to the Midwest to win support of the farmers. In the Canadian election, September 21, the Agreement and Sir Wilfrid Laurier and his Liberal government were defeated.

August 3   Signed arbitration treaties with France and England. Roosevelt was not in favor of them.

August 18   Taft vetoed tariff reductions on wool and woolen goods because the Tariff Board had not completed its investigation.

Fall   Left on Western tour, to take the issue of the arbitration treaties to the people. In March, 1912, the Senate confirmed watered-down treaties, which were not acceptable to England or France.

October 24   Suit filed against United States Steel for violating the Sherman Act. The suit contained the charge that Roosevelt had been deceived during the Panic of 1907, in allowing the corporation to purchase the Tennessee Coal & Iron Company. Roosevelt held Taft responsible for including this charge. This was the final blow to the friendship of Taft and Roosevelt. In March, 1920, the Supreme Court ruled in favor of United States Steel.

November 15   Attorney General Wickersham gave Taft Solicitor General Lehman's report on the National City Bank of New York. Wickersham and Lehman believed its investment subsidiary, The National City Company, was in violation of the National Banking Act. Taft, advised by Knox and MacVeigh, decided not to prosecute.

December   Tobacco Trust dissolved by order of the Supreme Court. Many thought the method of dividing it by tobacco products was injurious to the smaller businesses. Public opinion began to doubt the effectiveness of dissolution. (The heads of the trusts were never punished.) Andrew Carnegie, now retired, suggested government regulation of prices as the answer.

December 11   Taft sent to Congress the Tariff Board's 1200-page report on wool and woolen rates. Dr. F. W. Taussig, Harvard economist, in a critique of the report in March, 1912, stated that it was practically impossible to figure the cost of producing wool; that it varied from one region of the United States to the other and could not be a practical gauge in fixing tariffs. Cost was the basis of Taft's tariff theory.

1912

January 6   New Mexico admitted as forty-seventh state.

January 17   Taft urged the adoption of an annual budget for the United States government.
Taft's request for $250,000 for the continuance of the work of the Commission on Efficiency and Economy was lowered by Congress to $75,000 with the restriction that only three members could be paid over $4,000 a year. Many members were forced to resign.

January 18   Granted pardon to Charles W. Morse due to poor health. Morse had been convicted of misappropriating funds of the Bank of North America. In 1922 the then Attorney General Harry M. Daugherty was accused in the Senate of having conspired with another lawyer, T. B. Felder, for a large fee, to misrepresent Morse's health in order to gain his release. Morse survived Taft.

February 14   Arizona admitted as forty-eighth state.

February 22   Roosevelt made his "My hat is in the ring" speech in Ohio, in which he alienated Big Business by calling for the recall of judicial decisions.

March   Dr. Harvey W. Wiley, the head chemist for the Department of Agriculture, responsible for enforcing the Pure Food Act, resigned after difficulties with Secretary of Agriculture Wilson. Consumer groups and women's clubs were indignant and it became an issue in the 1912 election.

March 13   Mahlon Pitney took oath as Associate Justice of the Supreme Court.

March 27   First of the Japanese cherry trees planted in the capital by Mrs. Taft.

April 15   Appointed Julia Lathrop chief of the newly-created Children's Bureau at a salary of $5,000, the first woman appointed to such a responsible position.

June   Special message sent to Congress, which had refused to pass appropriation bills for government expenses.

June 22   Warren Harding of Ohio placed Taft's name in nomination at the Republican convention in Chicago. Roosevelt's backers had unsuccessfully contested the seating of regular party delegates. Chairman Elihu Root ruled that a delegate could vote on the question of other disputed seats but not his own. Taft received 561 votes; Roosevelt, 107; LaFollette, 41; Cummins, 17; Hughes, 2; with 344 abstaining. Sherman was renominated for Vice-president.

July 2   Woodrow Wilson nominated by Democrats on 46th ballot in Baltimore.

August 5   Theodore Roosevelt nominated for President by the Progressive Party (Bull Moose). George Perkins of International Harvester Company and publisher Frank Munsey provided the funds to form the party.

August 9   Taft vetoed a compromise tariff bill as "a bill identical with the one I vetoed before the report of the Tariff Board," whose recommendations were not followed.

August 24   Act passed providing Alaska with territorial government.
Signed a bill exempting American coastwise shipping from paying Panama Canal tolls. England, as well as many Americans, considered it a breach of the Hay-Pauncefote Treaty. In March, 1914, President Wilson requested that Congress repeal the exemptions, which it did.

September 34   U.S.S. Prairie, with 750 Marines, sent to Santo Domingo along with diplomatic request that law and order be restored and the treaty with the United States honored.

October 29   More United States battleships dispatched to Santo Domingo to restore order. President Victoria abdicated and was replaced by Archbishop Nouel.

October 30   Vice-president Sherman died. Nicholas Murray Butler, President of Columbia University, was chosen to replace him as the nominee.

November 5   Wilson elected President, with 6,286,214 popular votes; Roosevelt, 4,126,020; Taft, 3,483,922. Electoral votes: Wilson, 435; Roosevelt, 88; Taft, 8. Taft, surprised by his defeat and the number of votes Roosevelt received, felt that preventing Roosevelt's election ("the most dangerous man that we have had in this country since its origin") was the important thing.

December   Taft made an inspection trip to Panama.

1913

January 1   Parcel post service began.

February 14   Vetoed a bill that required a literacy test for entry into
                       the United States. The bill was favored by labor.

February 18   General Victoriano Huerta of Mexico headed a military
                       coup that overthrew Madero, who was then assassinated.
                       Taft, although urged by Americans who owned property
                       in Mexico to intervene, stood firm against United States
                       intervention.

February 25   Sixteenth Amendment ratified, giving Congress power
                       to collect taxes on income.

                       INTERIM

March 4   Woodrow Wilson inaugurated. In the afternoon Mr. and
                       Mrs. Taft left by train for a vacation in Augusta, Geor-
                       gia.

April 1   Returned to Yale where he had accepted a professorship
                       of law. In the next years, Taft was in great demand as
                       a speaker and also wrote articles for magazines, which
                       supplemented his $5,000 annual salary from Yale.

1914

March   Lunched at the White House with Wilson and Root. Had
                       a pleasant discussion.

July 28   Austria-Hungary declared war on Serbia.

August   Decided against running for Congress.

1915

January   In a lecture at the University of Virginia, Taft spoke on
                       "The Presidency," and criticized Roosevelt's broad-
                       ening the use of executive power. Taft said, ". . . our
                       President has no initiative in respect to legislation given

him by law, except that of mere recommendation, and no legal or formal method of entering into the argument and discussion of the proposed legislation while pending in Congress."

April

Taft and Roosevelt met for the first time since before the 1912 election, serving as pall bearers for Professor Thomas Lounsbury of Yale. The brief meeting was stiffly cordial.

June 17

The League to Enforce Peace was announced. Taft was named President. Hamilton Holt, William Howland and Theodore Marburg were among the proponents. The plan for the League included an international police force.

1916

March

Elihu Root, President of the American Bar Association, Taft and four other past presidents wrote to the Senate protesting Wilson's appointment of Louis B. Brandeis to the Supreme Court, declaring him not fit. He was confirmed by the Senate.

May 7

Lusitania sunk, with loss of 1198 lives including 114 Americans. Wilson did not protest to Germany, but made his "too proud to fight" speech in Philadelphia. Taft approved of Wilson's course. Roosevelt wanted German ships seized and commerce banned. Wilson did not accept Taft's suggestion to sever diplomatic relations.

May 15

The Democratic party was using Taft's pleas for support of Wilson in the war crisis as political ammunition against the Republican party. Taft became critical and questioned the administration's preparedness program and policies.

June

Charles Evans Hughes, Taft's choice for Republican nominee for president, was chosen. The Progressive

Party nominated Roosevelt, who declined. Taft and Roosevelt both campaigned for Hughes.

October 4   Taft and Roosevelt both attended a reception for Hughes at the Union League Club as an outward show of their reconciliation. Taft, however, still felt great animosity toward Roosevelt.

November   Wilson was re-elected, due in great part, thought Taft, to Roosevelt's extreme speeches.

1917

Fall   Taft and Frank P. Walsh named co-chairmen of the War Labor Conference Board, created to minimize labor problems in vital war industries.

December 12   Wilson dissuaded Taft from going to England to explain our policies and purpose in the war. The American ambassador to England, Walter H. Page, had suggested his going.

1918

March 28   Taft and A. Lawrence Lowell, President of Harvard University, conferred with Wilson regarding a proposed convention of the League to Enforce Peace with the British League of Nations Society. Wilson agreed that the conference should be held as long as details of a peace program were not discussed.

April 8   Named as joint chairman of the National War Labor Board, Taft moved to Washington. He took the position that yellow-dog contracts were against the policy of the board, although the Supreme Court had recently declared them legal and enforceable.

May   Taft and Roosevelt met by chance at the Blackstone Hotel. They reunited politically and successfully to help elect a Republican congress in November.

November 11   Armistice signed.

1919
January 5   Roosevelt died and Taft attended the funeral.

February   Toured through fifteen states trying to gain popular support for the League of Nations.

1920
March   League of Nations Treaty defeated for the second time in the Senate. Taft held Wilson responsible for its defeat because of his uncompromising attitude.

November   Warren Harding elected President over Democrat, James M. Cox. Taft was highly criticized by advocates for the League of Nations for supporting Harding.

SUPREME COURT JUSTICE

1921
June 30   Appointed Chief Justice of Supreme Court by President Harding.

December   As Chief Justice, Taft wrote report upholding the Interstate Commerce Commission and the Transportation Act of 1920; that Congress had the right to regulate interstate railroads even intrastate.

1922
May 15   Overruled the 1904 opinion of Chief Justice Edward Douglas White, regarding Congress's power of taxation, by disapproving a child labor law that imposed a 10% tax on the profits of companies using children.

1923
January   Pierce Butler of Minnesota, favored by Taft, was appointed by Harding to replace Justice William R. Day.

February   Judge Edward T. Sanford of the Circuit Court of Appeals chosen to replace Mahlon Pitney.

Taft said that the United States Railway Labor Board could determine who were the proper representatives of the workers. This helped make possible the Wagner-Connery Act of 1935.

August 2   President Harding died and Vice-president Calvin Coolidge became president.

1925

February 13   Judiciary Act, for which Taft had worked, passed, giving the Supreme Court greater power to decide which cases to hear.

1926

October   In Myers v. United States, Taft wrote what he considered one of his most important decisions. Taft said that senatorial agreement was not necessary for the dismissal of Frank S. Myers, an appointed postmaster of Portland, Oregon. The decision was 6 to 3, with Brandeis, McReynolds and Holmes dissenting. It was reversed by the Supreme Court of 1935.

1927

October 10   Supreme Court decided that the Elk Hills oil lease to Sinclair was fraudulent (Teapot Dome Scandal). Chief Justice Taft said, "The case presents one of the most outrageous instances of a conspiracy of silence . . . ."

1929

January 14   Read the decision in the Chicago Sanitary District case in its dispute with Wisconsin, Minnesota, Michigan and other states, found that the withdrawal of water from the Great Lakes by Chicago was to be limited to 4,167 cubic feet per second and ordered Chicago to begin immediate plans for sewage disposal plants.

March   Administered oath at inauguration of President Herbert Hoover.

| December 31 | Half brother Charles P. Taft died in Cincinnati, and although not feeling well, Taft insisted on attending the funeral, which weakened his resistance. |

1930

| February 3 | Taft sent his resignation as Chief Justice to President Hoover. |

| March 8 | Died at his home in Washington at 72 years of age. |

WILLIAM HOWARD TAFT ON THE INCOME TAX
June 16, 1909

In this special message to Congress, President Taft, shortly after his inauguration recommended un amendment to the Constitution giving the National Government the power to levy taxes on income. The amendment was proposed to the legislatures of the states by the Congress on July 2, 1909, and was ratified February 25, 1913.

To the Senate and House of Representatives:

It is the constitutional duty of the President from time to time to recommend to the consideration of Congress such measures as he shall judge necessary and expedient. In my inaugural address immediately preceding this present extraordinary session of Congress, I invited attention to the necessity for a revision of the tariff at this session, and stated the principles upon which I though the revision should be effected. I referred to the then rapidly increasing deficit, and pointed out the obligation on the part of the framers of the tariff bill to arrange the duty so as to secure an adequate income, and suggested that if it was not possible to do so by import duties, new kinds of taxation must be adopted, and among them I recommended a graduated inheritance tax as correct in principle and as certain and easy of collection. The House of Representatives has adopted the suggestion and has provided in the bill it passed for the collection of such a tax. In the Senate the action of its Finance Committee and the course of the debate indicate that it may not agree to this provision, and it is now proposed to make up the deficit by the imposition of a general income tax, in form and substance of almost exactly the same character as that which in the case of Pollock v. Farmers' Loan and Trust Company (157 U.S., 429) was held by the Supreme Court to be a direct tax, and therefore not within the power of the Federal Government to impose unless apportioned among the several States according to population. This new proposal, which I did not discuss in my inaugural address or in my message at the opening of the present session, makes it appropriate for me to submit to the Congress certain additional recommendations.

The decision of the Supreme Court in the income-tax cases deprived the National Government of a power which, by reason of previous decisions of the court, it was generally supposed that Government had. It is undoubtedly a power the National Government ought to have. It might be indispensable to the nation's life in great crises. Although I have not considered a constitutional amendment as necessary to the exercise of certain phases of this power, a mature consideration has satisfied me that an amendment is the only proper course for its establishment to its full extent. I therefore recommend to the Congress that both Houses, by a two-thirds vote, shall propose an amendment to the Constitution conferring the power to levy an income tax upon the National Government without apportionment among the States in proportion to population.

This course is much to be preferred to the one proposed of re-enacting a law once judicially declared to be unconstitutional. For the Congress to assume that the court will reverse itself, and to enact legislation on such an assumption, will not strengthen popular confidence in the stability of judicial construction of the Constitution. It is much wiser policy to accept the decision and remedy the defect by amendment in due and regular course.

Again, it is clear that by the enactment of the proposed law, the Congress will not be bringing money into the Treasury to meet the present deficiency, but by putting on the statute book a law already there and never repealed, will simply be suggesting to the executive officers of the Government their possible duty to invoke litigation. If the court should maintain its former view, no tax would be collected at all. If it should ultimately reverse itself, still no taxes would have been collected until after protracted delay.

It is said the difficulty and delay in securing the approval of three-fourths of the States will destroy all chance of adopting the amendment. Of course, no one can speak with certainty upon this point, but I have become convinced that a great majority of the people of this country are in favor of vesting the National Government with power to levy an income tax, and that they will secure the adoption of the amendment in the States, if proposed to them.

Second, the decision in the Pollock case left power in the National Government to levy an excise tax which accomplishes the same purpose as a corporation income tax, and is free from certain objections urged to the proposed income-tax measure.

I therefore recommend an amendment to the tariff bill imposing upon all corporations and joint stock companies for profit, except national banks (otherwise taxed), savings banks, and building and loan associations, an excise tax measured by 2 per cent. on the net income of such corporations. This is an excise tax upon the privilege of doing business as an artificial entity and of freedom from a general partnership liability enjoyed by those who own the stock.

I am informed that a 2 per cent. tax of this character would bring into the Treasury of the United States not less than $25,000,000.

The decision of the Supreme Court in the case of Spreckels Sugar Refining Company against McClain (192 U.S., 397) seems clearly to establish the principle that such a tax as this is an excise tax upon privilege and not a direct tax on property, and is within the federal power without apportionment according to population. The tax on net income is preferable to one proportionate to a percentage of the gross receipts, because it is a tax upon success and not failure. It imposes a burden at the source of the income at a time when the corporation is well able to pay and when collection is easy.

Another merit of this tax is the federal supervision which must be exercised in order to make the law effective over the annual accounts and business transactions of all corporations. While the faculty of assuming a corporate form has been of the utmost utility in the business world, it is also true that substantially all of the abuses and all of the evils which have aroused the public to the necessity of reform were made possible by the use of this very faculty. If now, by a perfectly legitimate and effective system of taxation we are incidentally able to possess the Government and the stockholders and the public of the knowledge of the real business transactions and the gains and profits of every corporation in the country, we have made a long step toward that supervisory control of corporations which may prevent a further abuse of power.

I recommend, then, first, the adoption of a joint resolution by two-thirds of both Houses proposing to the States an amendment to the Constitution granting to the Federal Government the right to levy and collect an income tax without apportionment among the States according to population, and, second, the enactment, as part of the pending revenue measure, either as a substitute for, or in addition to, the inheritance tax, of an excise tax upon all corporations measured by 2 per cent. of their net income.

WILLIAM H. TAFT

ADDRESS ON THE TARIFF LAW OF 1909

By President Taft at Winona, Minn., September 17, 1909.

My Fellow Citizens: As long ago as August, 1906, in the congressional campaign in Maine, I ventured to announce that I was a tariff revisionist and thought that the time had come for a readjustment of the schedules. I pointed out that it had been ten years prior to that time that the Dingley bill had been passed; that great changes had taken place in the conditions surrounding the productions of the farm, the factory, and the mine, and that under the theory of protection in that time the rates imposed in the Dingley bill in many instances might have become excessive; that is, might have been greater than the difference between the cost of production abroad and the cost of production at home with a sufficient allowance for a reasonable rate of profit to the American producer. I said that the party was divided on the issue, but that in my judgment the opinion of the party was crystallizing and would probably result in the near future in an effort to make such revision. I pointed out the difficulty that there always was in a revision of the tariff, due to the threatened disturbance of industries to be affected and the suspension of business, in a way which made it unwise to have too many revisions. In the summer of 1907 my position on the tariff was challenged, and I then entered into a somewhat fuller discussion of the matter. It was contended by by the so-called "standpatters" that rates beyond the necessary measure of protection were not objectionable, because behind the tariff wall competition always reduced the prices, and thus saved the consumer. But I pointed out in that speech what seems to me as true to-day as it then was, that the danger of excessive rates was in the temptation they created to form monopolies in the protected articles, and thus to take advantage of the excessive rates by increasing the prices, and therefore, and in order to avoid such a danger, it was wise at regular intervals to examine the question of what the effect of the rates had been upon the industries in this country, and whether the conditions with respect to the cost of production here had so changed as to warrant a reduction in the tariff, and to make a lower rate truly protective of the industry.

It will be observed that the object of the revision under such a statement was not to destroy protected industries in this country, but it was to continue to protect them where lower rates offered a sufficient protection to prevent injury by foreign competition. That was the object of the revision as advocated by me, and it was certainly the object of the revision as promised in the Republican platform.

I want to make as clear as I can this proposition, because, in order to determine whether a bill is a compliance with the terms of that platform, it must be understood what the platform means. A free trader is opposed to any protected rate because he thinks that our manufacturers, our farmers, and our miners ought to withstand the competition of foreign manufacturers and miners and farmers, or else go out of business and find something else more profitable to do. Now, certainly the promises of the platform did not contemplate the downward revision of the tariff rates to such a point that any industry theretofore protected should be injured. Hence, those who contend that the promise of the platform was to reduce prices by letting in foreign competition are contending for a free trade, and not for anything that they had the right to infer from the Republican platform.

The Ways and Means Committee of the House, with Mr. Payne at its head, spent a full year in an investigation, assembling evidence in reference to the rates under the tariff, and devoted an immense amount of work in the study of the question where the tariff rates could be reduced and where they ought to be raised with a view to maintaining a reasonably protective rate, under the principles of the platform, for every industry that deserved protection. They found that the determination of the question, what was the actual cost of production and whether an industry in this country could live under a certain rate and withstand threatened competition from abroad, was most difficult. The manufacturers were prone to exaggerate the injury which a reduction in the duty would give and to magnify the amount of duty that was needed; while the importers, on the other hand, who were interested in developing the importation from foreign shores, were quite likely to be equally biased on the other side.

Mr. Payne reported a bill — the Payne Tariff bill — which went to the Senate and was amended in the Senate by increasing the duty on some things and decreasing it on others. The difference between the House bill and the Senate bill was very much less than the newspapers represented. It turns out upon examination that the reductions in the Senate were about equal to those in the House, though they differed in character. Now, there is nothing quite so difficult as the discussion of a tariff bill, for the reason that it covers so many different items, and the meaning of the terms and the percentages are very hard to understand. The passage of a new bill, especially where a change in the method of assessing the duties has been followed, presents an opportunity for various modes and calculations of the percentages of increases and decreases that are most misleading and really throw no light at all upon the changes made. . . .

Attempts have been made to show what the real effect of these changes has been by comparing the imports under the various schedules, and assuming that the changes and their importance were in proportion to the importations. . . .

On the whole, however, I am bound to say that I think the Payne tariff bill is the best tariff bill that the Republican party ever passed; that in it the party has conceded the necessity for following the changed conditions and reducing tariff rates accordingly. This is a substantial achievement in the direction of lower tariffs and downward revision, and it ought to be accepted as such. Critics of the bill utterly ignore the very tremendous cuts that have been made in the iron schedule, which heretofore has been subject to criticism in all tariff bills. From iron ore, which was cut 75 per cent., to all the other items as low as 20 per cent., with an average of something like 40 or 50 per cent., that schedule has been reduced so that the danger of increasing prices through a monopoly of the business is very much lessened, and that was the chief purpose of revising the tariff downward under Republican protective principles. The severe critics of the bill pass this reduction in the metal schedule with a sneer, and say that the cut did not hurt the iron interests of the country. Well, of course it did not hurt them. It was not expected to hurt them. It was expected only to reduce excessive rates, so that business should still be conducted at a profit, and the very character of the criticism is an indication of the general injustice of the attitude of those who make it, in assuming that it was the promise of the Republican party to hurt the industries of the country by the reductions which they were to make in the tariff, whereas it expressly indicated as plainly as possible in the platform that all of the industries were to be protected against injury by foreign competition, and the promise only went to the reduction of excessive rates beyond what was necessary to protect them.

The high cost of living, of which 50 per cent. is consumed in food, 25 per cent. in clothing, and 25 per cent. in rent and fuel, has not been produced by the tariff, because the tariff has remained the same while the increases have gone on. It is due to the change of conditions the world over. Living has increased everywhere in cost — in countries where there is free trade and in countries where there is protection — and that increase has been chiefly seen in the cost of food products. In other words, we have had to pay more for the products of the farmer, for meat, for grain, for everything that enters into food. Now, certainly no one will contend that protection has increased the cost of food in this country, when the fact is that we have been the greatest exporters of food products in the world. It is only that the demand has increased beyond the supply, that farm lands have not been opened as rapidly as the population, and the demand has increased. I am not saying that the tariff does not increase prices in clothing and in building and in other items that enter into the necessities of life, but what I wish to emphasize is that the recent increases in the cost of living in this country have not been due to the tariff. We have a much higher standard of living in this country than they have abroad, and this has been made possible by higher income for the workingman, the farmer, and all classes. Higher wages have been made possible by the encouragement of diversified industries, built up and fostered by the tariff.

Now, the revision downward of the tariff that I have favored will not, I hope, destroy the industries of the country. Certainly it is not intended to. All that it is intended to do, and that is what I wish to repeat is to put the tariff where it will protect industries here from foreign competition, but will not enable those who will wish to monopolize to raise prices by taking advantage of excessive rates beyond the normal difference in the cost of production.

If the country desires free trade, and the country desires a revenue tariff and wishes the manufacturers all over the country to go out of business, and to have cheaper prices at the expense of the sacrifice of many of our manufacturing interests, then it ought to say so and ought to put the Democratic party in power if it thinks that party can be trusted to carry out any affirmative policy in favor of a revenue tariff. Certainly in the discussions in the Senate there was no great manifestation on the part of our Democratic friends in favor of reducing rates on necessities. They voted to maintain the tariff rates on everything that came from their particular sections. If we are to have free trade, certainly it can not be had through the maintenance of Republican majorities in the Senate and House and a Republican administration.

And now the question arises, what was the duty of a Member of Congress who believed in a downward revision greater than that which has been accomplished, who thought that the wool schedules ought to be reduced, and that perhaps there were other respects in which the bill could be improved? Was it his duty because, in his judgment, it did not fully and completely comply with the promises of the party platform as he interpreted it, and indeed as I had interpreted it, to vote against the bill? I am here to justify those who answer this question in the negative. Mr. Tawney was a downward revisionist like myself. He is a low-tariff man, and has been known to be such in Congress all the time he has been there. He is a prominent Republican, the head of the Appropriations Committee, and when a man votes as I think he ought to vote, and an opportunity such as this presents itself, I am glad to speak in behalf of what he did, not in defense of it, but in support of it.

This is a government by a majority of the people. It is a representative government. People select some 400 members to constitute the lower House and some 92 members to constitute the upper House through their legislatures, and the varying views of a majority of the voters in eighty or ninety millions of people are reduced to one resultant force to take affirmative steps in carrying on a government by a system of parties. Without parties popular government would be absolutely impossible. In a party, those who join it, if they would make it effective, must surrender their personal predilections on matters comparatively of less importance in order to accomplish the good which united action on the most important principles at issue secures.

Now, I am not here to criticise those Republican Members and Senators whose views on the subject of the tariff were so strong and intense that they believed it their duty to vote against their party on the tariff bill. It is a qestion for each man to settle for himself. The question is whether he shall help maintain the party solidarity for accomplishing its chief purposes, or whether the departure from principle in the bill as he regards it is so extreme that he must in conscience abandon the party. All I have to say is, in respect to Mr. Tawney's action, and in respect to my own in signing the bill, that I believed that the interests of the country, the interests of the party, required me to sacrifice the accomplishment of certain things in the revision of the tariff which I had hoped for, in order to maintain party solidarity, which I believe to be much more important than the reduction of rates in one or two schedules of the tariff. Had Mr. Tawney voted against the bill, and there had been others of the House sufficient in number to have defeated the bill, or if I had vetoed the bill because of the absence of a reduction of rates in the wool schedule, when there was a general downward revision, and a substantial one though not a complete one, we should have left the party in a condition of demoralization that would have prevented the accomplishment of purposes and a fulfillment of other promises which we had made just as solemnly as we had entered into that with respect to the tariff. When I could say without hesitation that this is the best tariff bill that the Republican party has ever passed, and therefore the best tariff bill that has been passed at all, I do not feel that I could have reconciled any other course to my conscience than that of signing the bill, and I think Mr. Tawney feels the same way. Of course, if I had vetoed the bill I would have received the applause of many Republicans who may be called low-tariff Republicans, and who think deeply on that subject, and of all the Democracy. Our friends the Democrats would have applauded, and then laughed in their sleeve at the condition in which the party would have been left; but, more than this, and waiving considerations of party, where would the country have been had the bill been vetoed or been lost by a vote? It would have left the question of the revision of the tariff open for further discussion during the next session. It would have suspended the settlement of all our business down to a known basis upon which prosperity could proceed and investments be made, and it would have held up the coming of prosperity to this country certainly for a year and probably longer. These are the reasons why I signed it.

But there are additional reasons why the bill ought not to have been beaten. It contained provisions of the utmost importance in the interest of this country in dealing with foreign countries and in the supplying of a deficit which under the Dingley bill seemed inevitable. There has been a disposition in some foreign countries taking advantage of greater elasticity in their systems of imposing tariffs and of making regulations to exclude our products and exercise against us undue discrimination. Against these things we have been helpless, because it required an act of Congress to meet the difficulties. It is now proposed by what is called the maximum and minimum clause, to enable the President to allow to come into operation a maximum or penalizing increase of duties over the normal or minimum duties whenever in his opinion the conduct of the foreign countries has been unduly discriminatory against the United States. It is hoped that very little use may be required of this clause, but its presence in the law and the power conferred upon the Executive, it is thought, will prevent in the future such undue discriminations. Certainly this is most important to our exporters of agricultural products and manufactures.

Second, We have imposed an excise tax upon corporations measured by 1 per cent. upon the net income of all corporations except fraternal and charitable corporations after exempting $5,000. This, it is thought, will raise an income of 26 to 30 millions of dollars, will supply the deficit which otherwise might arise without it, and will bring under federal supervision more or less all the corporations of the country. The inquisitorial provisions of the act are mild but effective, and certainly we may look not only for a revenue but for some most interesting statistics and the means of obtaining supervision over corporate methods that has heretofore not obtained.

Then, we have finally done justice to the Philippines. We have introduced free trade between the Philippines and the United States, and we have limited the amount of sugar and the amount of tobacco and cigars that can be introduced from the Philippines to such a figure as shall greatly profit the Philippines and yet in no way disturb the products of the United States or interfere with those engaged in the tobacco or sugar interests here. These features of the bill were most important, and the question was whether they were to be sacrificed because the bill did not in respect to wool and woolens and in some few other matters meet our expectations. I do not hesitate to repeat that I think it would have been an unwise sacrifice of the business interests of the country, it would have been an unwise sacrifice of the solidarity, efficiency, and promise-performing power of the party, to have projected into the next session another long discussion of the tariff, and to have delayed or probably defeated the legislation needed in the improvement of our interstate commerce regulation, and in making more efficient our antitrust law and the prosecutions under it. Such legislation is needed to clinch the Roosevelt policies, by which corporations and those in control of them shall be limited to a lawful path and shall be prevented from returning to those abuses which a recurrence of prosperity is too apt to bring about unless definite, positive steps of a legislative character are taken to mark the lines of honest and lawful corporate management.

Now, there is another provision in the new tariff bill that I regard as of the utmost importance. It is a provision which appropriates $75,000 for the President to employ persons to assist him in the execution of the maximum and minimum tariff clause and in the administration of the tariff law. Under that authority, I conceive that the President has the right to appoint a board, as I have appointed it, who shall associate with themselves and have under their control, a number of experts who shall address themselves, first, to the operation of foreign tariffs upon the exports of the United States, and then to the operation of the United States tariff upon imports and exports. There are provisions in the general tariff procedure for the ascertainment of the cost of production of articles abroad and the cost of production of articles here. I intend to direct the board in the course of these duties and in carrying them out, in order to assist me in the administration of the law, to make what might be called a glossary of the tariff, or a small encyclopedia of the tariff, or something to be compared to the United States Pharmacopoeia with reference to information as to drugs and medicines. I conceive that such a board may very properly, in the course of their duties, take up separately all the items of the tariff, both those on the free list and those which are dutiable, describe what they are, where they are manufactured, what their uses are, the methods of manufacture, the cost of production abroad and here, and every other fact with respect to each item which would enable the Executive to understand the operation of the tariff, the value of the article, and the amount of duty imposed, and all those details which the student of every tariff law finds it so difficult to discover. I do not intend, unless compelled or directed by Congress, to publish the result of these investigations, but to treat them merely as incidental facts brought out officially from time to time, and as they may be ascertained and put on record in the department, there to be used when they have all been accumulated and are sufficiently complete to justify executive recommendation based on them. Now, I think it is utterly useless, as I think it would be greatly distressing to business, to talk of another revision of the tariff during the present Congress. I should think that it would certainly take the rest of this administration to accumulate the data upon which a new and proper revision of the tariff might be had. By that time the whole Republican party can express itself again in respect to the matter and bring to bear upon its Representatives in Congress that sort of public opinion which shall result in solid party action. I am glad to see that a number of those who thought it their duty to vote against the bill insist that they are still Republicans and intend to carry on their battle in favor of lower duties and a lower revision within the lines of the party. That is their right and, in their view of things, is their duty.

It is vastly better that they should seek action of the party than that they should break off from it and seek to organize another party, which would probably not result in accomplishing anything more than merely defeating our party and inviting in the opposing party, which does not believe, or says that it does not believe, in protection. I think that we ought to give the present bill a chance. After it has been operating for two or three years, we can tell much more accurately than we can today its effect upon the industries of the country and the necessity for any amendment in its provisions.

I have tried to state as strongly as I can, but not more strongly than I think the facts justify, the importance of not disturbing the business interests of this country by an attempt in this Congress or the next to make a new revision; but meantime I intend, so far as in me lies, to secure official data upon the operation of the tariff, from which, when a new revision is attempted, exact facts can be secured.

I have appointed a tariff board that has no brief for either side in respect to what the rates shall be. I hope they will make their observations and note their data in their record with exactly the same impartiality and freedom from anxiety as to result with which the Weather Bureau records the action of the elements or any scientific bureau of the Government records the results of its impartial investigations. Certainly the experience in this tariff justifies the statement that no revision should hereafter be attempted in which more satisfactory evidence of an impartial character is not secured.

I am sorry that I am not able to go into further detail with respect to the tariff bill, but I have neither the information nor the time in which to do it. I have simply stated the case as it seemed to Mr. Tawney in his vote and as it seemed to me in my signing the bill.

FIRST ANNUAL MESSAGE
December 7, 1909

*In his first message to Congress on the State of
the Union,Taft covered foreign relations, government expenditures and revenues and other internal matters. This exerpt describes the deficit
on low magazine postage rates,and recommends
higher rates.This incurred the wrath of magazine
publishers and may have precipitated a decline
in his press relations.*

POST-OFFICE DEPARTMENT
Second-Class Mail Matter

The deficit every year in the Post-Office Department is largely
caused by the low rate of postage of 1 cent a pound charged on second-
class mail matter, which includes not only newspapers, but magazines
and miscellaneous periodicals. The actual loss growing out of the
transmission of this second-class mail matter at 1 cent a pound
amounts to about $63,000,000 a year. The average cost of the trans-
portation of this matter is more than 9 cents a pound.

It appears that the average distance over which newspapers are
delivered to their customers is 291 miles, while the average haul of
magazines is 1,049, and of miscellaneous periodicals 1,128 miles.
Thus, the average haul of the magazine is three and one-half times
and that of the miscellaneous periodical nearly four times the haul of
the daily newspaper, yet all of them pay the same postage rate of 1
cent a pound. The statistics of 1907 show that second-class mail
matter constituted 63.91 per cent. of the weight of all the mail, and
yielded only 5.19 per cent. of the revenue.

The figures given are startling, and show the payment by the
Government of an enormous subsidy to the newspapers, magazines,
and periodicals, and Congress may well consider whether radical
steps should not be taken to reduce the deficit in the Post-Office
Department caused by this discrepancy between the actual cost of
transportation and the compensation exacted therefor.

A great saving might be made, amounting to much more than half
of the loss, by imposing upon magazines and periodicals a higher rate
of postage. They are much heavier than newspapers, and contain a
much higher proportion of advertising to reading matter, and the
average distance of their transportation is three and ahalf times as
great.

The total deficit for the last fiscal year in the Post-Office Department amounted to $17,500,000. The branches of its business which it
did at a loss were the second-class mail service, in which the loss,
as already said, was $63,000,000, and the free rural delivery, in which
the loss was $28,000,000. These losses were in part offset by the

profits of the letter postage and other sources of income. It would seem wise to reduce the loss upon second-class mail matter, at least to the extent of preventing a deficit in the total operations of the Post-Office.

I commend the whole subject to Congress, not unmindful of the spread of intelligence which a low charge for carrying newspapers and periodicals assists. I very much doubt, however, the wisdom of a policy which constitutes so large a subsidy and requires additional taxation to meet it. . . .

SECOND ANNUAL MESSAGE

THE WHITE HOUSE, December 6, 1910.

To the Senate and House of Representatives:

During the past year the foreign relations of the United States have continued upon a basis of friendship and good understanding.

ARBITRATION

The year has been notable as witnessing the pacific settlement of two important international controversies before the Permanent Court of The Hague.

The arbitration of the Fisheries dispute between the United States and Great Britain, which has been the source of nearly continuous diplomatic correspondence since the Fisheries Convention of 1818, has given an award which is satisfactory to both parties. This arbitration is particularly noteworthy not only because of the eminently just results secured, but also because it is the first arbitration held under the general arbitration treaty of April 4, 1908, between the United States and Great Britain, and disposes of a controversy the settlement of which has resisted every other resource of diplomacy, and which for nearly ninety years has been the cause of friction between two countries whose common interest lies in maintaining the most friendly and cordial relations with each other.

The United States was ably represented before the tribunal. The complicated history of the questions arising made the issue depend, more than ordinarily in such cases, upon the care and skill with which our case was presented, and I should be wanting in proper recognition of a great patriotic service if I did not refer to the lucid historical analysis of the facts and the signal ability and force of the argument — six days in length — presented to the Court in support of our case by Mr. Elihu Root. As Secretary of State, Mr. Root had given close study to the intricate facts bearing on the controversy, and by diplomatic correspondence had helped to frame the issues. At the solicitation of the Secretary of State and myself, Mr. Root, though burdened by his duties as Senator from New York, undertook the preparation of the case as leading counsel, with the condition imposed by himself that, in view of his position as Senator, he should not receive any compensation.

The Tribunal constituted at The Hague by the Governments of the United States and Venezuela has completed its deliberations and has rendered an award in the case of the Orinoco Steamship Company against Venezuela. The award may be regarded as satisfactory since it has, pursuant to the contentions of the United States, recognized a number of important principles making for a judicial attitude in the determining of international disputes.

In view of grave doubts which had been raised as to the constitutionality of The Hague Convention for the establishment of an International Prize Court, now before the Senate for ratification, because of that provision of the Convention which provides that there may be an appeal to the proposed Court from the decisions of national courts, this government proposed in an Identic Circular Note addressed to those Powers who had taken part in the London Maritime Conference, that the powers signatory to the Convention, if confronted with such difficulty, might insert a reservation to the effect that appeals to the International Prize Court in respect to decisions of its national tribunals, should take the form of a direct claim for compensation; that the proceedings thereupon to be taken should be in the form of a trial de novo, and that judgment of the Court should consist of compensation for the illegal capture, irrespective of the decision of the national court whose judgment had thus been internationally involved. As the result of an informal discussion it was decided to provide such procedure by means of a separate protocol which should be ratified at the same time as the Prize Court Convention itself.

Accordingly, the Government of the Netherlands, at the request of this Government, proposed under date of May 24, 1910, to the powers signatory to The Hague Convention, the negotiation of a supplemental protocol embodying stipulations providing for this alternative procedure. It is gratifying to observe that this additional protocol is being signed without objection, by the powers signatory to the original convention, and there is every reason to believe that the International Prize Court will be soon established.

The Identic Circular Note also proposed that the International Prize Court when established should be endowed with the functions of an Arbitral Court of Justice under and pursuant to the recommendation adopted by the last Hague Conference. The replies received from the various powers to this proposal inspire the hope that this also may be accomplished within the reasonably near future.

It is believed that the establishment of these two tribunals will go a long way toward securing the arbitration of many questions which have heretofore threatened and, at times, destroyed the peace of nations.

PEACE COMMISSION

Appreciating these enlightened tendencies of modern times, the Congress at its last session passed a law providing for the appointment of a commission of five members "to be appointed by the President of the United States to consider the expediency of utilizing existing international agencies for the purpose of limiting the armaments of the nations of the world by international agreement, and of constituting the combined navies of the world an international force for the preservation of universal peace, and to consider and report upon any other means to diminish the expenditures of government for military purposes and to lessen the probabilities of war."

I have not as yet made appointments to this Commission because I have invited and am awaiting the expressions of foreign governments as to their willingness to cooperate with us in the appointment of similar commissions or representatives who would meet with our commissioners and by joint action seek to make their work effective.

GREAT BRITAIN AND CANADA

Several important treaties have been negotiated with Great Britain in the past twelve months. A preliminary diplomatic agreement has been reached regarding the arbitration of pecuniary claims which each Government has against the other. This agreement, with the schedules of claims annexed, will, as soon as the schedules are arranged, be submitted to the Senate for approval.

An agreement between the United States and Great Britain with regard to the location of the international boundary line between the United States and Canada in Passamaquoddy Bay and to the middle of Grand Manan Channel was reached in a Treaty concluded May 21, 1910, which has been ratified by both Governments and proclaimed, thus making unnecessary the arbitration provided for in the previous treaty of April 11, 1908.

The Convention concluded January 11, 1909, between the United States and Great Britain providing for the settlement of international differences between the United States and Canada including the apportionment between the two countries of certain of the boundary waters and the appointment of Commissioners to adjust certain other questions has been ratified by both Governments and proclaimed.

The work of the International Fisheries Commission appointed in 1908, under the treaty of April 11, 1908, between Great Britain and the United States, has resulted in the formulation and recommendation of uniform regulations governing the fisheries of the boundary waters of Canada and the United States for the purpose of protecting and increasing the supply of food fish in such waters. In completion of this work, the regulations agreed upon require congressional legislation to make them effective and for their enforcement in fulfillment of the treaty stipulations.

PORTUGAL

In October last the monarchy in Portugal was overthrown, a provisional Republic was proclaimed, and there was set up a de facto Government which was promptly recognized by the Government of the United States for purposes of ordinary intercourse pending formal recognition by this and other Powers of the Governmental entity to be duly established by the national sovereignty.

LIBERIA

A disturbance among the native tribes of Liberia in a portion of the Republic during the early part of this year resulted in the sending, under the Treaty of 1862, of an American vessel of war to the disaffected district, and the Liberian authorities, assisted by the good offices of the American Naval Officers, were able to restore order. The negotiations which have been undertaken for the amelioration of the conditions found in Liberia by the American Commission, whose report I transmitted to Congress on March 25 last, are being brought to conclusion, and it is thought that within a short time practical measures of relief may be put into effect through the good offices of this Government and the cordial cooperation of other governments interested in Liberia's welfare.

THE NEAR EAST
TURKEY

To return the visit of the Special Embassy announcing the accession of his Majesty Mehemet V, Emperor of the Ottomans, I sent to Constantinople a Special Ambassador who, in addition to this mission of ceremony, was charged with the duty of expressing to the Ottoman Government the value attached by the Government of the United States to increased and more important relations between the countries and the desire of the United States to contribute to the larger economic and commercial development due to the new regime in Turkey.

The rapid development now beginning in that ancient empire and the marked progress and increased commercial importance of Bulgaria, Roumania, and Servia make it particularly opportune that the possibilities of American commerce in the Near East should receive due attention.

MONTENEGRO

The National Skoupchtina having expressed its will that the Principality of Montenegro be raised to the rank of Kingdom, the Prince of Montenegro on August 15 last assumed the title of King of Montenegro. It gave me pleasure to accord to the new kingdom the recognition of the United States.

THE FAR EAST

The center of interest in Far Eastern affairs during the past year has again been China.

It is gratifying to note that the negotiations for a loan to the Chinese Government for the construction of the trunk railway lines from Hankow southward to Canton and westward through the Yangtse Valley, known as the Hukuang Loan, were concluded by the representatives of the various financial groups in May last and the results approved by their respective governments. The agreement, already initialed by the Chinese Government, is now awaiting formal ratification. The basis of the settlement of the terms of this loan was one of exact equality between America, Great Britain, France, and Germany in respect to financing the loan and supplying materials for the proposed railways and their future branches.

The application of the principle underlying the policy of the United States in regard to the Hukuang Loan, viz., that of the internationalization of the foreign interest in such of the railways of China as may be financed by foreign countries, was suggested on a broader scale by the Secretary of State in a proposal for internationalization and commercial neutralization of all the railways of Manchuria. While the principle which led to the proposal of this Government was generally admitted by the powers to whom it was addressed, the Governments of Russia and Japan apprehended practical difficulties in the execution of the larger plan which prevented their ready adherence. The question of constructing the Chinchow-Aigun railway by means of an international loan to China is, however, still the subject of friendly discussion by the interested parties.

The policy of this Government in these matters has been directed by a desire to make the use of American capital in the development of China an instrument in the promotion of China's welfare and material prosperity without prejudice to her legitimate rights as an independent political power.

This policy has recently found further exemplification in the assistance given by this Government to the negotiations between China and a group of American bankers for a loan of $50,000,000 to be employed chiefly in currency reform. The confusion which has from ancient times existed in the monetary usages of the Chinese has been one of the principal obstacles to commercial intercourse with that people. The United States in its Treaty of 1903 with China obtained a pledge from the latter to introduce a uniform national coinage, and the following year, at the request of China, this Government sent to Peking a member of the International Exchange Commission, to discuss with the Chinese Government the best methods of introducing the reform. In 1908 China sent a Commissioner to the United States to consult with American financiers as to the possibility of securing a large loan with which to inaugurate the new currency system, but the death of Their Majesties, the Empress Dowager and the Emperor of China, interrupted the negotiations, which were not resumed until a few months ago, when this Government was asked to communicate to the bankers concerned the request of China for a loan of $50,000,000 for the purpose under review. A preliminary agreement between the American group and China has been made covering the loan.

For the success of this loan and the contemplated reforms which are of the greatest importance to the commercial interests of the

United States and the civilized world at large, it is realized that an expert will be necessary, and this Government has received assurances from China that such an adviser, who shall be an American, will be engaged.

It is a matter of interest to Americans to note the success which is attending the efforts of China to establish gradually a system of representativo government. The provincial assemblies were opened in October, 1909, and in October of the present year a consultative body, the nucleus of the future national parliament, held its first session at Peking.

The year has further been marked by two important international agreements relating to Far Eastern affairs. In the Russo-Japanese Agreement relating to Manchuria, signed July 4, 1910, this Government was gratified to note an assurance of continued peaceful conditions in that region and the reaffirmation of the policies with respect to China to which the United States together with all other interested powers are alike solemnly committed.

The treaty annexing Korea to the Empire of Japan, promulgated August 29, 1910, marks the final step in a process of control of the ancient empire by her powerful neighbor that has been in progress for several years past. In communicating the fact of annexation the Japanese Government gave to the Government of the United States assurances of the full protection of the rights of American citizens in Korea under the changed conditions.

Friendly visits of many distinguished persons from the Far East have been made during the year. Chief among these were Their Imperial Highnesses Princes Tsai-tao and Tsai-Hsun of China; and His Imperial Highness Prince Higashi Fushimi, and Prince Tokugawa, President of the House of Peers of Japan. The Secretary of War has recently visited Japan and China in connection with his tour to the Philippines, and a large delegation of American business men are at present traveling in China. This exchange of friendly visits has had the happy effect of even further strengthening our friendly international relations.

LATIN AMERICA

During the past year several of our southern sister Republics celebrated the one hundredth anniversary of their independence. In honor of these events, special embassies were sent from this country to Argentina, Chile, and Mexico, where the gracious reception and splendid hospitatlity extended them manifested the cordial relations and freindship existing between those countries and the United States, relations which I am happy to believe have never before been upon so high a plane and so solid a basis as at present.

The Congressional commission appointed under a concurrent resolution to attend the festivities celebrating the centennial anniversary of Mexican independence, together with a special ambassador, were received with the highest honors and with the greatest cordiality, and returned with the report of the bounteous hospitality and warm reception of President Diaz and the Mexican people, which left no doubt of the desire of the immediately neighboring Republic to continue the mutually beneficial and intimate relations which I feel sure the two governments will ever cherish. . . .

ANNUAL MESSAGE — PART I.

On the Anti-Trust Statute.

December 5, 1911

To the Senate and House of Representatives:

This message is the first of several which I shall send to Congress during the interval between the opening of its regular session and its adjournment for the Christmas holidays. The amount of information to be communicated as to the operations of the Government, the number of important subjects calling for comment by the Executive, and the transmission to Congress of exhaustive reports of special commissions, make it impossible to include in one message of a reasonable length a discussion of the topics that ought to be brought to the attention of the National Legislature at its first regular session.

THE ANTI-TRUST LAW-THE SUPREME COURT DECISIONS

In May last the Supreme Court handed down decisions in the suits in equity brought by the United States to enjoin the further maintenance of the Standard Oil Trust and of the American Tobacco Trust, and to secure their dissolution. The decisions are epoch-making and serve to advise the business world authoritatively of the scope and operation of the anti-trust act of 1890. The decisions do not depart in any substantial way from the previous decisions of the court in construing and applying this important statute, but they clarify those decisions by further defining the already admitted exceptions to the literal construction of the act. By the decrees, they furnish a useful precedent as to the proper method of dealing with the capital and property of illegal trusts. These decisions suggest the need and wisdom of additional or supplemental legislation to make it easier for the entire business community to square with the rule of action and legality thus finally established and to preserve the benefit, freedom, and spur of reasonable competition without loss of real efficiency or progress.

NO CHANGE IN THE RULE OF DECISION —
MERELY IN ITS FORM OF EXPRESSION

The statute in its first section declares to be illegal "every contract, combination in the form of trust or otherwise, or conspiracy, in restraint of trade or commerce among the several States or with foreign nations," and in the second, declares guilty of a misdemeanor "every person who shall monopolize or attempt to monopolize or combine or conspire with any other person to monopolize any part of the trade or commerce of the several States or with foreign nations."

In two early cases, where the statute was invoked to enjoin a transportation rate agreement between interstate railroad companies, it was held that it was no defense to show that the agreement as to rates complained of was reasonable at common law, because it was said that the statute was directed against all contracts and combinations in restraint of trade whether reasonable at common law or not. It was plain from the record, however, that the contracts complained of in those cases would not have been deemed reasonable at common law. In subsequent cases the court said that the statute should be given a reasonable construction and refused to include within its inhibition, certain contractual restraints of trade which it denominated as incidental or as indirect.

These cases of restraint of trade that the court excepted from the operation of the statute were instances which, at common law, would have been called reasonable. In the Standard Oil and Tobacco cases, therefore, the court merely adopted the tests of the common law, and in defining exceptions to the literal application of the statute, only substituted for the test of being incidental or indirect, that of being reasonable, and this, without varying in the slightest the actual scope and effect of the statute. In other words, all the cases under the statute which have now been decided would have been decided the same way if the court had originally accepted in its construction the rule at common law.

It has been said that the court, by introducing into the construction of the statute common-law distinctions, has emasculated it. This is obviously untrue. By its judgment every contract and combination in restraint of interstate trade made with the purpose or necessary effect of controlling prices by stifling competition, or of establishing in whole or in part a monopoly of such trade, is condemned by the statute. The most extreme critics can not instance a case that ought to be condemned under the statute which is not brought within its terms as thus construed.

The suggestion is also made that the Supreme Court by its decision in the last two cases has committed to the court the undefined and unlimited discretion to determine whether a case of restraint of trade is within the terms of the statute. This is wholly untrue. A reasonable restraint of trade at common law is well understood and is clearly defined. It does not rest in the discretion of the court. It must be limited to accomplish the purpose of a lawful main contract to which, in order that it shall be enforceable at all, it must be incidental. If it exceed the needs of that contract, it is void.

The test of reasonableness was never applied by the court at common law to contracts or combinations or conspiracies in restraint of trade whose purpose was or whose necessary effect would be to stifle competition, to control prices, or establish monopolies. The courts never assumed power to say that such contracts or combinations or conspiracies might be lawful if the parties to them were only moderate in the use of the power thus secured and did not exact from the public too great and exorbitant prices. It is true that many theorists, and others engaged in business violating the statute, have hoped that some such line could be drawn by courts; but no court of authority has ever attempted it. Certainly there is nothing in the decisions of the latest two cases from which such a dangerous theory of judicial discretion in enforcing this statute can derive the slightest sanction.

FORCE AND EFFECTIVENESS OF STATUTE A MATTER OF GROWTH

We have been twenty-one years making this statute effective for the purposes for which it was enacted. The Knight case was discouraging and seemed to remit to the States the whole available power to attack and supress the evils of the trusts. Slowly, however, the error of that judgment was corrected, and only in the last three or four years has the heavy hand of the law been laid upon the great illegal combinations that have exercised such an absolute dominion over many of our industries. Criminal prosecutions have been brought and a number are pending, but juries have felt averse to convicting for jail sentences, and judges have been most reluctant to impose such sentences on men of respectable standing in society whose offense has been regarded as merely statutory. Still, as the offense becomes better understood and the committing of it partakes more of studied and deliberate defiance of the law, we can be confident that juries will convict individuals and that jail sentences will be imposed.

THE REMEDY IN EQUITY BY DISSOLUTION

In the Standard Oil case the Supreme and Circuit Courts found the combination to be a monopoly of the interstate business of refining, transporting, and marketing petroleum and its products, effected and maintained through thirty-seven different corporations, the stock of which was held by a New Jersey company. It in effect commanded the dissolution of this combination, directed the transfer and pro rata distribution by the New Jersey company of the stock held by it in the thirty-seven corporations to and among its stockholders; and the corporations and individual defendants were enjoined from conspiring or combining to restore such monopoly; and all agreements between the subsidiary corporations tending to produce or bring about further violations of the act were enjoined.

In the Tobacco case, the court found that the individual defendants, twenty-nine in number, had been engaged in a successful effort to acquire complete dominion over the manufacture, sale, and distribution of tobacco in this country and abroad, and that this had been done by combinations made with a purpose and effect to stifle competition, control prices, and establish a monopoly, not only in the manufacture of tobacco, but also of tin-foil and licorice used in its manufacture and of its products of cigars, cigarettes, and snuffs. The tobacco suit presented a far more complicated and difficult case than the Standard Oil suit for a decree which would effectuate the will of the court and end the violation of the statute. There was here no single holding company as in the case of the Standard Oil Trust. The main company was the American Tobacco Company, a manufacturing, selling, and holding company. The plan adopted to destroy the combination and restore competition involved the redivision of the capital and plants of the whole trust between some of the companies constituting the trust and new companies organized for the purposes of the decree and made parties to it, and numbering, new and old, fourteen.

SITUATION AFTER READJUSTMENT

The American Tobacco Company (old), readjusted capital, $92,-000,000; the Liggett & Meyers Tobacco Company (new), capital, $7,000,000; the P. Lorillard Company (new), capital, $47,000,000; and the R.J. Reynolds Tobacco Company (old), capital, $7,525,000, are chiefly engaged in the manufacture and sale of chewing and smoking tobacco and cigars. The former one tin-foil company is divided into two, one of $825,000 capital and the other of $400,000. The one snuff company is divided into three companies, one with a capital of $15,000,-000, another with a capital of $8,000,000, and a third with a capital of $8,000,000. The licorice companies are two, one with a capital of $5,758,300 and another with a capital of $2,000,000. There is, also, the British-American Tobacco Company, a British corporation, doing business abroad with a capital of $26,000,000, the Porto Rican Tobacco Company, with a capital of $1,800,000, and the corporation of United Cigar Stores, with a capital of $9,000,000.

Under this arrangement, each of the different kinds of business will be distributed between two or more companies with a division of the prominent brands in the same tobacco products, so as to make competition not only possible but necessary. Thus the smoking-tobacco business of the country is divided so that the present independent companies have 21.39 per cent, while the American Tobacco Company will have 33.08 per cent, the Liggett & Meyers 20.05 per cent, the Lorillard Company 22.82 per cent, and the Reynolds Company 2.66 per cent. The stock of the other thirteen companies, both preferred and common, has been taken from the defendant American Tobacco Company and has been distributed among its stockholders. All covenants restricting competition have been declared null and further performance of them has been enjoined. The perferred stock of the different companies has now been given voting power which was denied it under the old organization. The ratio of the preferred stock to the common was as 78 to 40. This constitutes a very decided change in the character of the ownership and control of each company.

In the original suit there were twenty-nine defendants who were charged with being the conspirators through whom the illegal combination acquired and exercised its unlawful dominion. Under the decree these defendants will hold amounts of stock in the various distributee companies ranging from 41 per cent as a maximum to 28-1/2 per cent as a minimum, except in the case of one small company, the Porto Rican Tobacco Company, in which they will hold 45 per cent. The twenty-nine individual defendants are enjoined for three years from buying any stock except from each other, and the group is thus prevented from extending its control during that period. All parties to the suit, and the new companies who are made parties, are enjoined perpetually from in any way effecting any combination between any of the companies in violation of the statute by way of resumption of the old trust. Each of the fourteen companies is enjoined from acquiring stock in any of the others. All these companies are enjoined from having common directors or officers, or common buying or selling agents, or common offices, or lending money to each other.

SIZE OF NEW COMPANIES

Objection was made by certain independent tobacco companies that this settlement was unjust because it left companies with very large capital in active business, and that the settlement that would be effective to put all on an equality would be a division of the capital and plant of the trust into small fractions in amount more nearly equal to that of each of the independent companies. This contention results from a misunderstanding of the anti-trust law and its purpose. It is not intended thereby to prevent the accumulation of large capital in business enterprises in which such a combination can secure reduced cost of production, sale, and distribution. It is directed against such an aggregation of capital only when its purpose is that of stifling competition, enchancing or controlling prices, and establishing a monopoly. If we shall have by the decree defeated these purposes and restored competition between the large units into which the capital and plant have been divided, we shall have accomplished the useful purpose of the statute.

CONFISCATION NOT THE PURPOSE OF THE STATUTE

It is not the purpose of the statute to confiscate the property and capital of the offending trusts. Methods of punishment by fine or imprisonment of the individual offenders, by fine of the corporation or by forfeiture of its goods in transportation, are provided, but the proceeding in equity is a specific remedy to stop the operation of the trust by injunction and prevent the future use of the plant and capital in violation of the statute.

EFFECTIVINESS OF DECREE

I venture to say that not in the history of American law has a decree more effective for such a purpose been entered by a court than that agaist the Tobacco Trust. As Circuit Judge Noyes said in his judgment approving the decree:

> "The extent to which it has been necessary to tear apart this combination and force it into forms with the attendant burdens ought to demonstrate that the Federal anti-trust statute is a drastic statute which accomplishes effective results; which so long as it stands on the statute books must be obeyed, and which can not be disobeyed without incurring far-reaching penalties. And, on the other hand, the successful reconstruction of this organization should teach that the effect of enforcing this statute is not to destroy, but to reconstruct; not to demolish, but to re-create in accordance with the conditions which the Congress has declared shall exist among the people of the United States."

COMMON STOCK OWNERSHIP

It has been assumed that the present pro rata and common ownership in all these companies by former stockholders of the trust would insure a continuance of the same old single control of all the companies into which the trust has by decree been disintegrated. This is erroneous and is based upon the assumed inefficacy and innocuousness of judicial injunctions. The companies are enjoined from co-operation or combinabination; they have different managers, directors, purchasing and sales agents. If all or many of the numerous stockholders, reaching into the thousands, attempt to secure concerted action of the companies with a view to the control of the market, their number is so large that such an attempt could not well be concealed, and its prime movers and all its participants would be at once subject to contempt proceedings and imprisonment of a summary character. The immediate result of the present situation will necessarily be activity by all the companies under different managers, and then competition must follow, or there will be activity by one comapny and stagnation by another. Only a short time will inevitably lead to a change in ownership of the stock, as all opportunity for continued co-operation must disappear. Those critics who speak of this disintegration in the trust as a mere change of garments have not given consideration to the inevitable working of the decree and understand little the personal danger of attempting to evade or set at naught the solemn injunction of a court whose object is made plain by the decree and whose inhibitions are set forth with a detail and comprehensiveness unexampled in the history of equity jurisprudence.

VOLUNTARY REORGANIZATIONS
OF OTHER TRUSTS AT HAND

The effect of these two decisions has led to decrees dissolving the combination of manufacturers of electric lamps, a southern wholesale grocers' association, an interlocutory decree against the Powder Trust with directions by the circuit court compelling dissolution, and other combinations of a similar history are now negotiating with the Department of Justice looking to a disintegration by decree and reorganization in accordance with law. It seems possible to bring about these reorganizations without general business distrubance.

MOVEMENT FOR REPEAL OF THE ANTI-TRUST LAW

But now that the anti-trust act is seen to be effective for the accomplishment of the purpose of its enactment, we are met by a cry from many different quarters for its repeal. It is said to be obstructive of business progress, to be an attempt to restore old-fashioned methods of destructive competition between small units, and to make impossible those useful combinations of capital and the reduction of the cost of production that are essential to continued prosperity and normal growth.

In the recent decisions the Supreme Court makes clear that there is nothing in the statute which condemns combinations of capital or mere bigness of plant organized to secure economy in production and a reduction of its cost. It is only when the purpose or necessary effect of the organization and maintenance of the combination or the aggregation of immense size are the stifling of competition, actual and potential, and the enhancing of prices and establishing a monopoly, that the statute is violated. Mere size is no sin against the law. The merging of two or more business plants necessarily eliminates competition between the units thus combined, but this elimination is in contravention of the statute only when the combination is made for purpose of ending this particular competition in order to secure control of, and enhance, prices and create a monopoly.

LACK OF DEFINITENESS IN THE STATUTE

The complaint is made of the statute that it is not sufficiently definite in its description of that which is forbidden, to enable business men to avoid its violation. The suggestion is, that we may have a combination of two corporations, which may run on for years, and that subsequently the Attorney General may conclude that it was a violation of the statute, and that which was supposed by the combiners to be innocent then turns out to be a combination in violation of the statute. The answer to this hypothetical case is that when men attempt to amass such stupendous capital as will enable them to supress competition, control prices and establish a monopoly, they know the purpose of their acts. Men do not do such a thing without having it clearly in mind. If what they do is merely for the purpose of reducing the cost of production, without the thought of suppressing competition by use of the bigness of the plant they are creating, then they can not be convicted at the time the union is made, nor can they be convicted later, unless it happen that later on they conclude to suppress competition and take the usual methods for doing so, and thus establish for themselves a monopoly. They can, in such a case, hardly complain if the motive which subsequently is disclosed is attributed by the court to the original combination.

NEW REMEDIES SUGGESTED

Much is said of the repeal of this statute and of constructive legislation intended to accomplish the purpose and blaze a clear path for honest merchants and business men to follow. It may be that such a plan will be evolved, but I submit that the discussions which have been brought out in recent days by the fear of the continued execution of the anti-trust law have produced nothing but glittering generalities and have offered no line of distinction or rule of action as definite and as clear as that which the Supreme Court itself lays down in enforcing the statute.

SUPPLEMENTAL LEGISLATION NEEDED – NOT REPEAL OR AMENDMENT

I see no objection – and indeed I can see decided advantages – in the enactment of a law which shall describe and denounce methods of competition which are unfair and are badges of the unlawful purpose denounced in the anti-trust law. The attempt and purpose to suppress a competitor by underselling him at a price so unprofitable as to drive him out of business, or the making of exclusive contracts with customers under which they are required to give up association with other manufacturers, and numerous kindred methods for stifling competition and effecting monopoly, should be described with sufficient accuracy in a criminal statute on the one hand to enable the Government to shorten its task by prosecuting single misdemeanors instead of an entire conspiracy, and, on the other hand, to serve the purpose of pointing out more in detail to the business community what must be avoided.

FEERAL INCORPORATION RECOMMENDED

In a special message to Congress on January 7, 1910, I ventured to point out the disturbance to business that would probably attend the dissolution of these offending trusts. I said:

> "But such an investigation and possible prosecution of corporations whose prosperity or destruction affects the comfort not only of stockholders but of millions of wage earners, employees, and associated tradesmen must necessarily tend to disturb the confidence of the business community, to dry up the now flowing sources of capital from its places of hoarding, and produce a halt in our present

prosperity that will cause suffering and strained circumstances among the innocent many for the faults of the guilty few. The question which I wish in this message to bring clearly to the consideration and discussion of Congress is whether, in order to avoid such a possible business danger, something can not be done by which these business combinations may be offered a means, without great financial disturbance, of changing the character, organization, and extent of their business into one within the lines of the law under Federal control and supervision, securing compliance with the anti-trust statute.

"Generally, in the industrial combinations called 'trusts,' the principal business is the sale of goods in many States and in foreign markets; in other words, the interstate and foreign business far exceeds the business done in any one State. This fact will justify the Federal Government in granting a Federal charter to such a combination to make and sell in interstate and foreign commerce the products of useful manufacture under such limitations as will secure a compliance with the anti-trust law. It is possible so to frame a statute that while it offers protection to a Federal company against harmful, vexations, and unnecessary invasion by the States, it shall subject it to reasonable taxation and control by the States with respect to its purely local business.

"Corporations organized under this act should be prohibited from acquiring and holding stock in other corporations (except for special reasons, upon approval by the proper Federal authority), thus avoiding the creation under national auspices of the holding company with subordinate corporations in different States, which has been such an effective agency in the creation of the great trusts and monopolies.

"If the prohibition of the anti-trust act against combinations in restraint of trade is to be effectively enforced, it is essential that the National Government shall provide for the creation of national corporations to carry on a legitmate business throughout the United States. The conflicting laws of the different States of the Union with respect to foreign corporations make it difficult, if not impossible, for one corporation to comply with their requirements so as to carry on business in a number of different States."

I renew the recommendation of the enactment of a general law providing for the voluntary formation of corporations to engage in trade and commerce among the States and with foreign nations.

Every argument which was then advanced for such a law, and every explanation which was at that time offered to possible objections, have been confirmed by our experience since the enforcement of the anti-trust statute has resulted in the actual dissolution of active commercial organizations.

It is even more manifest now than it was then that the denunciation of conspiracies in restraint of trade should not and does not mean the denial of organizations large enough to be intrusted with our interstate and foreign trade. It has been made more clear now than it was then that a purely negative statute like the anti-trust law may well be supplemented by specific provisions for the building up and regulation of legitimate national and foreign commerce.

GOVERNMENT ADMINISTRATIVE EXPERTS NEEDED TO AID COURTS IN TRUST DISSOLUTIONS

The drafting of the decrees in the dissolution of the present trusts, with a view to their reorganization into legitimate corporations, has made it especially apparent that the courts are not provided with the administrative machinery to make the necessary inquiries preparatory to reorganization, or to pursue such inquiries, and they should be empowered to invoke the aid of the Bureau of Corporations in determining the suitable reorganization of the disintegrated parts: The circuit court and the Attorney General were greatly aided in framing the decree in the Tobacco Trust dissolution by an expert from the Bureau of Corporations.

FEDERAL CORPORATION COMMISSION PROPOSED

I do not set forth in detail the terms and sections of a statute which might supply the constructive legislation permitting and aiding the formation of combinations of capital into Federal corporations. They should be subject to rigid rules as to their organization and procedure, including effective publicity, and to the closest supervision as to the issue of stock and bonds by an executive bureau or commission in the Department of Commerce and Labor, to which in times of doubt they might well submit their proposed plans for future business, It must be distinctly understood that incorporation under Federal law could not exempt the company thus formed and its incorporators and managers from prosecution under the anti-trust law for subsequent illegal conduct, but the publicity of its procedure and the opportunity for frequent consultation with the bureau or commission in charge of the incorporation as to the legitimate purpose of its transactions would offer it as great security against successful prosecutions for violations of the law as would be practical or wise.

Such a bureau or commission might well be invested also with the duty already referred to, of aiding courts in the dissolution and re-creation of trusts within the law. It should be an executive tribunal of the dignity and power of the Comptroller of the Currency or the Interstate Commerce Commission, which now exercise supervisory power over important classes of corporations under Federal regulation.

The drafting of such a Federal incorporation law would offer ample opportunity to prevent many manifest evils in corporate management to-day, including irresponsibility of control in the hands of the few who are not the real owners.

INCORPORATION VOLUNTARY

I recommend that the Federal charters thus to be granted shall be voluntary, at least until experience justifies mandatory provisions. The benefit to be derived from the operation of great business under the protection of such a charter would attract all who are anxious to keep within the lines of the law. Other large combinations that fail to take advantage of the Federal incorporation will not have a right to complain if their failure is ascribed to unwillingness to submit their transactions to the careful official scrutiny, competent supervision, and publicity attendant upon the enjoyment of such a charter.

ONLY SUPPLEMENTAL LEGISLATION NEEDED

The opportunity thus suggested for Federal incorporation, it seems to me, is suitable constructive legislation needed to facilitate the squaring of great industrial enterprises to the rule of action laid down by the anti-trust law. This statute as construed by the Supreme Court must continue to be the line of distinction for legitimate business. It must be enforced, unless we are to banish individualism from all business and reduce it to one common system of regulation or control of prices like that which now prevails with respect to public utilities, and which when applied to all business would be a long step toward State socialism.

IMPORTANCE OF THE ANTI-TRUST ACT

The anti-trust act is the expression of the effort of a freedom-loving people to preserve equality of opportunity. It is the result of the confident determination of such a people to maintain their future growth by preserving uncontrolled and unrestricted the enterprise of the individual, his industry, his ingenuity, his intelligence, and his independent courage.

For twenty years or more this statute has been upon the statute book. All knew its general purpose and approved. Many of its violators were cynical over its assumed impotence. It seemed impossible of enforcement. Slowly the mills of the courts ground, and only gradually did the majesty of the law assert itself. Many of its statesmen-authors died before it became a living force, and they and others saw the evil grow which they had hoped to destroy. Now its efficacy is seen; now its power is heavy; now its object is near achievement. Now we hear the call for its repeal on the plea that it interferes with business prosperity, and we are advised in most general terms, how by some other statute and in some other way the evil we are just stamping out can be cured, if we only abandon this work of twenty years and try another experiment for another term of years.

It is said that the act has not done good. Can this be said in the face of the effect of the Northern Securities decree? That decree was in no way so drastic or inhibitive in detail as either the Standard Oil decree or the Tobacco decree; but did it not stop for all time the then powerful movement toward the control of all the railroads of the country in a single hand? Such a one-man power could not have been a healthful influence in the Republic, even though exercised under the general supervision of an interstate commission.

Do we desire to make such ruthless combinations and monopolies lawful? When all energies are directed, not toward the reduction of the cost of production for the public benefit by a healthful competition, but toward new ways and means for making permanent in a few hands the absolute control of the conditions and prices prevailing in the whole field of industry, then individual enterprise and effort will be paralyzed and the spirit of commercial freedom will be dead.

WM. H. TAFT.

SPECIAL MESSAGE

On economy and efficiency in the Government service.

THE WHITE HOUSE, January 17, 1912

To the Senate and House of Representatives:

I submit for the information of the Congress this report of progress made in the inquiry into the efficiency and economy of the methods of transacting public business.

Efficiency and economy in the Government service have been demanded with increasing insistence for a generation. Real economy is the result of efficient organization. By perfecting the organization the same benefits may be obtained at less expense. A reduction in the total of the annual appropriations is not in itself a proof of economy, since it is often accompanied by a decrease in efficiency. The needs of the Nation may demand a large increase of expenditure, yet to keep the total appropriations within the expected revenue is necessary to the maintenance of public credit.

Upon the President must rest a large share of the responsibility for the demands made upon the Treasury for the current administration of the executive branch of the Government. Upon the Congress must rest responsibility for those grants of public funds which are made for other purposes.

REASON FOR THE INQUIRY

Recognizing my share of responsibility for efficient and economical administration, I have endeavored during the past two years, with the assistance of heads of departments, to secure the best results. As one of the means to this end I requested a grant from Congress to make my efforts more effective.

An appropriation of $100,000 was made June 25, 1910, "to enable the President to inquire into the methods of transacting the public business of the executive departments and other Government establishments and to recommend to Congress such legislation as may be necessary to carry into effect changes found to be desirable that can not be accomplished by Executive action alone." I have been given this fund to enable me to take action and to make specific recommendations with respect to the details of transacting the business of an organization whose activities are almost as varied as those of the entire business world. The operations of the Government affect the interest of every person living within the jurisdiction of the United States. Its organization embraces stations and centers of work located in every city and in many local subdivisions of the country. Its gross expenditures amount to nearly $1,000,000,000 annually. Including the personnel of the Military and Naval Establishments, more than

400,000 persons are required to do the work imposed by law upon the executive branch of the Government.

MAGNITUDE OF THE TASK

This vast organization has never been studied in detail as one piece of administrative mechanism. Never have the foundations been laid for a thorough consideration of the relations of all of its parts. No comprehensive effort has been made to list its multifarious activities or to group them in such a way as to present a clear picture of what the Government is doing. Never has a complete description been given of the agencies through which these activities are performed. At no time has the attempt been made to study all of these activities and agencies with a view to the assignment of each activity to the agency best fitted for its performance, to the avoidance of duplication of plant and work, to the integration of all administrative agencies of the Government, so far as may be practicable, into a unified organization for the most effective and economical dispatch of public business.

FIRST COMPLETE INVESTIGATION

Notwithstanding that voluminous reports are compiled annually and presented to the Congress, no satisfactory statement has ever been published of the financial transactions of the Government as a whole. Provision is made for due accountability for all moneys coming into the hands of officers of the Government, whether as collectors of revenue or disbursing agents, and for insuring that authorizations for expenditures as made by law shall not be exceeded. But no general system has ever been devised for reporting and presenting information regarding the character of the expenditures made, in such a way as to reveal the actual costs entailed in the operation of individual services and in the performance of particular undertakings; nor in such a way as to make possible the exercise of intelligent judgment regarding the discretion displayed in making expenditure and concerning the value of the results obtained when contrasted with the sacrifices required. Although earnest efforts have been put forth by administrative officers and though many special inquiries have been made by the Congress, no exhaustive investigation has ever before been instituted concerning the methods employed in the transaction of public business with a view to the adoption of the practices and procedure best fitted to secure the transaction of such business with maximum dispatch, economy, and efficiency.

With large interests at stake the Congress and the Administration have never had all the information which should be currently available if the most intelligent direction is to be given to the business in hand.

I am convinced that results which are really worth while can not be secured, or at least can be secured only in small part, through the prosecution at irregular intervals of special inquiries bearing on particular services or features of administration. The benefits thus obtained must be but temporary. The problem of good administration is not one that can be solved at one time. It is a continuously present one.

PLAN OF THE WORK

In accordance with my instructions, the Commission on Economy and Efficiency, which I organized to aid me in the inquiry, has directed its efforts primarily to the formulation of concrete recommendations looking to the betterment of the fundamental conditions under which government operations must be carried on. With a basis thus laid, it has proceeded to the prosecution of detailed studies of individual services and classes of work, and of particular practices and methods, pushing these studies as far, and covering as many points and services, as the resources and time at its disposal have permitted.

In approaching its task it has divided the work into five fields of inquiry having to do respectively with organization, personnel, business methods, accounting and reporting, and the budget.

ORGANIZATION

I have stated that the Congress, the President, and the administrative officers are attempting to discharge the duties with which they are intrusted without full information as to the agencies through which the work of the Government is being performed. To provide more complete information on this point the commission has submitted to me a report on the organization of the Government as it existed July 1, 1911. This report, which is transmitted herewith, shows in great detail, by means of outlines, not only the departments, commissions, bureaus, and offices through which the Government performs its varied activities, but also the sections, shops, field stations, etc., constituting the subordinate divisions through which the work is actually done. It shows for the services at Washington each such final unit as a laboratory, library, shop, and administrative subdivision; and for the services outside of Washington each station and point at which any activity of the Government is carried on.

OUTLINES OF ORGANIZATION

From these outlines it is possible to determine not only how each department, bureau, and operating unit, such as a navy yard, is organized, but also, by classifying these units by character and geographical location, the number of units of a like character that exist at Washington, and the number and character of services of the Government in each city or other point in the United States. With this information available, it is possible to study any particular activity or the problem of maintaining services at any given city or point.

Information of this character has never before been available. Administrative officials have been called upon to discharge their duties without that full knowledge of the machinery under their direction which is so necessary to the exercise of effective control; much less have they had information regarding agencies in other services that might be made use of. Under such circumstances each service is compelled to rely upon itself, to build up its own organization, and to provide its own facilities regardless of those in existence elsewhere.

This outline has been prepared on the loose-leaf system, so that it is possible to keep it revised to date at little or no expense. The outline thus constitutes a work of permanent value.

COMPREHENSIVE PLAN OF ORGANIZATION

With this outline as a basis, the commission has entered upon the preparation of three series of reports. The first series deals with the manner in which the services of the Government should be grouped in departments. This is a matter of fundamental importance. It is only after a satisfactory solution of this problem that many important measures of reform become possible. Only by grouping services according to their character can substantial progress be made in eliminating duplication of work and plant and proper working relations be established between services engaged in similar activities. Until the head of a department is called upon to deal exclusively with matters falling in but one or a very few distinct fields, effective supervision and control is impossible. As long as the same department embraces services so diverse in character as those of life saving and the management of public finances, standardization of accounting methods and of other business practices is exceedingly difficult of attainment.

So dependent are other reforms upon the proper grouping of services that I have instructed the commission to indicate in its report the changes which should be made in the existing organization and to proceed in the same way as would far-seeing architects or engineers in planning for the improvement and development of a great city. My desire is to secure and to furnish to the Congress a scheme of organization that can be used as a basis of discussion and action for years to come.

In the past services have been created one by one as exigencies have seemed to demand, with little or no reference to any scheme of organization of the Government as a whole. I am convinced that the time has come when the Government should take stock of all its activities and agencies and formulate a comprehensive plan with reference to which future changes may be made. The report of the commission is being prepared with this idea in mind. When completed it will be transmitted to the Congress. The recommendations will be of such a character that they can be acted upon one by one if they commend themselves to the Congress and as action in regard to any one of them is deemed to be urgent.

EFFORTS ON PARTICULAR SERVICES

The second and third series of reports deal, respectively, with the organization and activities of particular services, and the form of organization for the performance of particular business operations.

One of the reports of the second series is upon the Revenue-Cutter Service, which costs the Government over two and a half million dollars each year. In the opinion of the commission its varied activities can be performed with equal, or greater, advantage by other services. The commission, therefore, recommends that it be abolished. It is estimated that by so doing a saving of not less than $1,000,000 a year can be made.

Another report illustrating the second series recommends that the Lighthouse and Life-Saving Services be administered by a single bureau instead of as at present by two bureaus located in different departments. These services have much in common. Geographically, they are similarly located; administratively, they have many of the same problems. It is estimated that consolidation would result in a saving of not less than $100,000 annually.

In a third report the commission has recommended the abolition of the Returns Office of the Department of the Interior. This action, in its opinion, will cause no loss in service to the public and will result in a direct saving of not less than $25,000 a year, in addition to a large indirect economy in the reduction of work to be performed in the several offices.

In another report the commission has recommended the consolidation of the six auditing offices of the Treasury and the inclusion in the auditing system of the seven naval officers who now audit customs accounts at the principal ports. The changes recommended will improve in many ways the auditing of public accounts and will result in an immediate saving of at least $135,000 annually.

GENERAL TECHNICAL SERVICES

A third series of reports is being prepared on those branches of the organization which are technical in character and which exist for the service of the Government as a whole — branches which have to do with such matters as public printing, heating, lighting, the making of repairs, the providing of transportation, and the compilation of statistics where mechanical equipment is essential.

ABOLITION OF LOCAL OFFICES

Perhaps the part of the organization in which the greatest economy in public expenditure is possible is to be found in the numerous local offices of the Government. In some instances the establishment and the discontinuance of the local offices are matters of administrative discretion. In other instances they are established by permanent law in such a manner that their discontinuance is beyond the power of the President or that of any executive officer. In a number of services these laws were passed nearly a century ago. Changes in economic conditions have taken place which have had the effect of rendering certain offices not only useless but even worse than useless in that their very existence needlessly swells expenditures and complicates the administrative system.

The attention of the Congress has been called repeatedly to these conditions. In some instances the Congress has approved recommendations for the abolition of useless positions. In other cases not only do the recommendations of the Executive that useless positions be abolished remain unheeded, but laws are passed to establish new offices at places where they are not needed.

The responsibility for the maintenance of these conditions must naturally be divided between the Congress and the Executive. But that the Executive has performed his duty when he has called the attention of the Congress to the matter must also be admitted. Realizing my responsibility in the premises, I have directed the commission to prepare a report setting forth the positions in the local services of the Government which may be discontinued with advantage, the saving which would result from such action and the changes in law which are necessary to carry into effect changes in organization found to be desirable. On the coming in of the report, such offices as may be found useless and can be abolished will be so treated by Executive order.

PERSONNEL

In my recent message to the Congress I urged consideration of the necessity of placing in the classified service all of the local officers under the Departments of the Treasury, the Interior, Post Office, and Commerce and Labor.

CLASSIFICATION OF LOCAL OFFICERS

The importance of the existence of a competent and reasonably permanent civil service was not appreciated until the last quarter of the last century. At that time examinations were instituted as a means of ascertaining whether candidates for appointment possessed the requisite qualifications for Government positions. Since then it has come to be universally admitted that entrance to almost every subordinate position in the public service should be dependent upon the proof in some appropriate way of the ability of the appointee.

As yet, however, little if any attempt has been made by law to secure, either for the higher administrative positions in the service at

Washington or for local offices, the qualifications which the incumbents of these positions must have if the business of the Government is to be conducted in the most efficient and economical manner. Furthermore, in the case of many of the local officers the law positively provides that the term of office shall be of four years' duration.

The next step which must be taken is to require of heads of bureaus in the departments at Washington, and of most of the local officers under the departments, qualifications of capacity similar to those now required of certain heads of bureaus and of local officers. The extension of the merit system to these officers and a needed readjustment of salaries will have important effects in securing greater economy and efficiency.

In the first place, the possession by the incumbents of these positions of the requisite qualifications must in itself promote efficiency.

In the second place, the removal of local officers from the realm of political patronage in many cases would reduce the pay roll of the field services. At the present time the incumbents of many of these positions leave the actual performance of many of their duties to deputies and assistants. The Government often pays two persons for doing work that could easily be done by one. What is the loss to the Government can not be stated, but that it is very large can not be denied, when it is remembered how numerous are the local officers in the postal, customs, internal revenue, public lands, and other field services of the Government.

In the third place, so long as local officers are within the sphere of political patronage it is difficult to consider the question of the establishment or discontinuance of local offices apart from the effect upon local poltical situations.

Finally, the view that these various offices are to be filled as a result of political considerations has for its consequence the necessity that the President and Members of Congress devote to matters of patronage time which they should devote to questions of policy and administration.

The greatest economy and efficiency, and the benefits which is most worth while, may be assured only by treating all the distinctly administrative officers in the departments at Washington and in the field in the same way as inferior officers have been treated. The time has come when all these officers should be placed in the classified service. The time has also come when those provisions of law which give to these officers a fixed term of years should be repealed. So long as a fixed term is provided by law the question of reappointment of an officer, no matter how efficiently he may have performed his duties, will inevitably be raised periodically. So long as appointments to these offices must be confirmed by the Senate, and so long as appointments to them must be made every four years, just so long will it be impossible to provide a force of employees with a reasonably permanent tenure who are qualified by reason of education and training to do the best work.

SUPERANNUATION

Attention has been directed in recent years to the need of a suitable plan of retiring the superannuated employees in the executive civil service. In the belief that it is desirable that any steps toward the establishment of such a plan shall be taken with caution, I instructed the commission to make an inquiry first into the conditions at Washington. This inquiry has been directed to the ascertainment of the extent to which superannuation now exists and to the consideration of the availability of the various plans which either have been proposed for adoption in this country or have actually been adopted in other countries. I shall submit, in the near future, for the consideration of the Congress a plan for the retirement of aged employees in the civil service which will safeguard the interests of the Government and at the same time make reasonable provision for the needs of those who have given the best part of their lives to the service of the State.

EFFICIENCY OF PERSONNEL

I have caused inquiry to be made into the character of the appointees from the point of view of efficiency and competence which has resulted from present methods of appointment; into the present relation of compensation to the character of work done; into the existing methods of promotion and the keeping of efficiency records in the various departments; and into the conditions of work in Government offices. This inquiry will help to determine to what extent conditions of work are uniform in the different departments and how far uniformity in such conditions will tend to improve the service. I have felt that satisfaction with the conditions in which they worked was a necessary prerequisite to an efficient personnel, and that satisfaction was not to be expected where conditions in one department were less favorable than in another.

This inquiry has not been completed. When it has been ascertained that evils exist which can be remedied through the exercise of the powers now vested in the President, I shall endeavor to remedy those evils. Where that is not the case, I shall present for the consideration of the Congress plans which, I believe, will be followed by great improvement in the service.

BUSINESS METHODS

In every case where technical processes have been studied it has been demonstrated beyond question that large economies may be effected. The subjects first approached were those which lie close to each administrator, viz, office practices. An illustration of the possibilities within this field may be found in the results of the inquiry into the methods of handling and filing correspondence. Every office in the Government has reported its methods to the commission. These reports brought to light the fact that present methods were quite the reverse of uniform. Some offices follow the practice of briefing all correspondence; some do not. Some have flat files; others fold all papers before filing. Some use press copies; other retain only carbon copies.

UNNECESSARY COST OF HANDLING
AND FILING CORRESPONDENCE

The reports also show not only a very wide range in the methods of doing this comparatively simple part of the Government business, but an extraordinary range in cost. For the handling of incoming mail the averages of cost by departments vary from $5.85 to $81.40 per 1,000. For the handling of outgoing mail the averages by departments vary from $5.94 to $69.89 per 1,000. This does not include the cost of preparation, but is confined merely to the physical side of the work. The variations between individual offices is many times greater than that shown for averages by departments.

It is at once evident either that it is costing some of the offices too little or that others are bing run at an unwarranted expense. Nor are these variations explained by differences in character of work. For example, there are two departments which handle practically the same kind of business and in very large volume. The average cost of handling incoming mail to one was found to be over six times as great as the cost of handling incoming mail to the other.

It has been found that differences of average cost by departments closely follow differences in method and that the greatest cost is found in the department where the method is most involved. Another fact is of interest, viz, that in two departments, which already show low averages, orders have been issued which will lead to a large saving without impairing efficiency. It can not be said what the saving ultimately will be when the attention of officers in all of the departments has been focused on present methods with a view to changing them in such manner as to reduce cost to the lowest point compatible with efficient service. It, however, must be a considerable percentage of nearly $5,000,000, the total estimated cost of handling this part of the Government business at Washington.

Results have already been obtained which are noteworthy. Mention has been made of the orders issued by two departments. Of these the order of one is most revolutionary in character, since it requires flat filing, where before all correspondence was folded; the doing away with letterpress copies; and the discontinuance of indorsements on slips, one of the most expensive processes and one which in the other department has been carried to very great length.

NEED FOR LABOR-SAVING OFFICE DEVICES

The use of labor-saving office devices in the service has been made the subject of special inquiry. An impression prevails that the Government is not making use of mechanical devices for economizing labor to the same extent as are efficiently managed private enterprises. A study has been made of the extent to which devices of this character are now being employed in the several branches of the Government and the opportunities that exist for their more general use. In order to secure information as to the various kinds of labor-saving devices that are inexistence and as to their adaptability to Government work. an exhibition of labor-saving office appliances was held in Washington from July 6 to 15, 1911. One hundred and ten manufacturers and dealers participated, and more than 10,000 officers and employees visited the exhibition. There is no doubt that the exhibition served the purpose of bringing to the attention of officers devices which can be employed by them with advantage. The holding of this exhibition was, however, but a step preparatory to the contemplated investigation.

UNNECESSARY COST OF COPY WORK

The efforts of the commission resulted also in the adoption by several bureaus or departments of improved methods of doing copying. The amount of copy work heretofore done by hand each year in the many offices is estimated to aggregate several hundred thousand dollars. The commission exhibited, at its offices, appliances that were thought to be especially adapted to this kind of Government work. Following these demonstrations methods of copying were introduced which have brought about a saving of over 75 per cent in offices where used for six months. This change in one small cross section of office practice will more than offset the whole cost of my inquiry.

WASTE IN THE DISTRIBUTION OF PUBLIC DOCUMENTS

Going outside the office, one of the business processes which have been investigated is the distribution of departmental documents. This is a subject with which both the Congress and Administration heads are familiar. The prevailing practice in handling departmental publications is to have them manufactured at the Government Printing Office; each job when completed is delivered to the department; here the books or pamphlets are wrapped and addressed; they are then sent to the post office; there they are assorted and prepared for shipment through the mails; from the post office they are sent to the railroad station, which is only a few steps from the Government Printing Office whence they started. The results of this laborious and circuitous method is to make the use of the best mechanical equipment impracticable and to waste each year not less than a quarter of a million dollars of Government funds in useless handling, to say nothing of the indirect loss due to lack of proper coordination.

WASTEFUL USE OF PROPERTIES AND EQUIPMENT

The use of equipment is a matter which also has been investigated. Up to the present time this investigation has been in the main confined to the subject of electric lighting. The Government pays over $600,000 per year for electric current; it has made large capital outlays for wiring and fixtures. With the increasing demands in many buildings the present equipment is taxed to its limit and if the present methods are continued much of this wiring must be done over; in many places employees are working at a great physical disadvantage, due to inadequate and improper lighting, and thereby with reduced efficiency. In every place where the inquiry has been conducted it appears that there is large waste; that without the cost of rewiring, simply by giving proper attention to location of lights and the use of proper lamps and reflectors, the light efficiency at points where needed may be much increased and the cost of current reduced from 30 to 60 per cent. Other inquiries into the use which is being made of properties and equipment are contemplated which promise even larger results.

UNNECESSARY COST OF INSURANCE

It is the policy of the Government not to insure public property against fire and other losses. Question has been raised whether the Government might not apply the same principle to other forms of risk, including insurance of the fidelity of officials and employees. A report is now in preparation on the subject which will show opportunities for large savings. I believe that the present expense for insuring the faithful execution of contracts, which, though paid by the contractor, is more than covered in the added price to the Government, can be largely reduced without taking away any element of security.

LACK OF SPECIFICATIONS

The importance of establishing and maintaining standard specifications is found not only in the possibility of very materially reducing the direct cost of Government trading, but also in insuring to the service materials, supplies, and equipment which are better adapted to its purposes. One of the results of indefiniteness of specifications is to impose contract conditions which make it extra-hazardous for persons to enter into contractual relations. This not only deprives the Government of the advantage of broad competition, but causes it to pay an added margin in price to vendors who must carry the risk. The specifications which may have been worked out in one department usually differ from specifications for the same article to be used in another department. Much progress has been made toward improving this condition through the schedules of the General Supply Committee, but there are many classes of supplies not on these lists which may be standardized, and the articles which are there listed may be specified with exactness.

In connection with standard specifications for purchasing, the subject of a standard form of contract has been given consideration. No one form or small number of forms will be applicable to all the agreements into which the Government enters. There can be standard conditions and provisions for such contracts, however, and the work in this connection is being prosecuted in an effort to simplify the forms of contracts and to do away with the great diversity of requirements which so often perplex and irritate those who wish to enter into a contract with the Government.

EXCESSIVE COST OF TRAVEL

One of the first steps taken toward constructive work was the reclassification of the expenditures for the year 1910 by objects. The foundation was thus made for the investigation of Government trading practices. While it was recognized that this large field could not be covered within a year except at enormous cost, the subjects of "Transportation of persons" and "Subsistence while in travel status" were taken as concrete examples. The annual cost of travel to the Government was found to be about $12,000,000. It was also found that the Government employees were traveling in practically every way that was open to the public; it was further found that although the Government was the largest user of transportation, it was buying railroad tickets on a less favorable basis than would be possible if the subject of traveling expenditures were systematically handled from the point of view of the Government as a whole. The form of ticket most often used between such points as New York, Philadelphia, and Washington was the single-trip first-class ticket. In two departments definite tests have been made in the use of mileage books and in each practically the same result has been reported, viz., an average saving of a little over one-half of 1 cent per mile. What the possible saving to the Government by a more systematic handling of transportation may be, can not be estimated at this time. Upon inquiry it was found that an analysis of travel vouchers for the year would cost not less than $120,000. The investigation, therefore, was confined to the analysis of travel vouchers which came to departments during the month of April. A report of the result of this inquiry has been made and at an early date will be sent to the Congress with recommendations.

One of the results or by-products of this inquiry into travel expenses was the recommendation that the jurat or affidavit which is now required by order of the comptroller be discontinued. The jurat does not add to the value of the return, involves persons traveling in much annoyance and trouble in going before an officer competent to administer oaths, while every disciplinary result is obtained through certification under the law prescribing a penalty for the falsification of accounts. A discontinuance of the jurat in all cases would result in a direct saving of about $60,000 per annum.

OTHER EXPENDITURES TO BE INVESTIGATED

Before economy in Government trading can be adequately covered, such subjects as the following must be systematically inquired into, viz.: Subsistence and support of persons; subsistence and care for animals and the storage and care of vehicles; telephone, telegraph, and commercial messenger service; printing, engraving, lithographing, and binding; advertising and the publication of notices; heat, light, power, and electricity purchased; repairs by contract and open market order; building and other materials; drafting, scientific and stationery supplies; fuel; mechanics', engineering, and electricians' supplies; cleaning and toilet supplies; wearing apparel and hand-sewing supplies; forage and other supplies for animals; provisions; explosives and pyrotechnic supplies; heat, light, power, and electrical equipment; live stock; furniture and furnishings; educational and scientific equipment. From what has been already ascertained concerning certain of these different objects of Government expenditure, it is evident that large savings will result from such an examination.

BETTER METHODS FOR PURCHASING

Through a long period of years and by numerous laws and orders there has grown up a procedure governing public advertising and contracting that is more burdensome and expensive in some cases than is necessary. The procedure is not uniform in the various departments; it is not uniform in many cases for the different services in the same department. To make uniform the requirements so far as practicable will be in the interest of economy and efficiency and bring about that simplicity that will secure the largest opportunity for contractors to bid for Government work, and will secure for the Government the most favorable prices obtained by any purchaser.

ACCOUNTING AND REPORTING

In my message of March 3, 1911, attention was called to some of the defects in the present methods of accounting and reporting. I said:

> The condition under which legislators and administrators, both past and present, have been working may be summarized as follows: There have been no adequate means provided whereby either the President or his advisers may act with intelligence on current business before them; there has been no means for getting prompt, accurate, and correct information as to results obtained; * * * there have been practically no accounts showing what the Government owns and only a partial representation of what it owes; appropriations have been over encumbered without the facts being known; officers of Government have had no regular or systematic method of having brought to their attention the costs of governmental administration, operation, and main-

tenance, and therefore could not judge as to economy or waste; there has been inadequate means whereby those who served with fidelity and efficiency might make a record of accomplishment and be distinguished from those who were inefficient and wasteful; functions and establishments have been duplicated, even multiplied, causing conflict and unnecessary expense; lack of full information has made intelligent direction impossible and cooperation between different branches of the service difficult.

By reason of the confused character of records and reports and the lack of information which has been provided, this was one of the first subjects into which inquiry was made looking toward the issuing of Executive orders.

CHARACTER OF ACCOUNTS REQUIRED

In laying the foundation for the revision of the present accounting methods it has been assumed that such information should be produced, and only such as is continuously needed by administrative heads or as will be of value to the Congress. The work has been prosecuted under the following heads: The character and form of expenditure documents that should be employed by the several departments; classification of objects of expenditure; the kind and character of accounts that should be kept by the Government; the character of reports giving information regarding revenues and expenditures that should be rendered to superior administrative officers and to the Congress, and which will enable them to lay before the Congress information which each Member should have in order that the legislative branch may be fully informed concerning the objects and purposes of governmental expenditures.

UNIFORMITY IN CLASSIFICATION AND METHODS

Upon these matters the commission has made extended studies. So far as the kind and character of accounts to be kept by the Government are concerned, not only have reports on methods of accounting and reporting been made by representatives of each of the departments, but for four of these services detailed descriptive reports have been prepared showing exactly what forms are used and what procedure is followed in keeping and recording accounts. Proceeding from these statements of fact, the purpose is to work out in collaboration with department representatives a unified procedure, and a uniform classification of facts which will enable accounting officers to present to administrative heads, to the President, and to the Congress complete, accurate, and prompt information, in any summary or detail that may be desired.

CONSTRUCTIVE RESULTS OBTAINED

The general basis for uniformity of accounting and reporting has already been laid in constructive reports with recommendations. The results of this work have been promulgated by the Comptroller of the Treasury with the approval of the Secretary of the Treasury in circulars issued in May and June last. These circulars prescribed the kind of accounts which shall be kept for the purpose of making available to the administrative head of each department, bureau, and office the information which is needed for directing the business of the Government.

In all of the work of the commission on these subjects emphasis has been laid upon cooperation with departmental committees composed of representatives appointed by the heads of departments for the express purpose of joining with the commission in the preliminary studies and in the conclusions and recommendations relating to the several departments and establishments.

REPORTS AT PRESENT REQUIRED BY CONGRESS

During the consideration of these subjects the commission has made a study of the present requirements of law relating to reports which are in whole or in part financial in character from the various departments and establishments. There are more than 90 acts of Congress which annually require reports of this character. These requirements of the law result in nearly 200 printed reports relating to financial matters, which must be submitted annually to the Congress by the various departments and establishments. Studies of these reports and comparisons of the classification of expenditures as set forth therein have been made by the commission to the end that, so far as practicable, uniformity of classification of objects of expenditure may be recommended and identical terminology adopted.

RECOMMENDATIONS AND MODIFICATIONS

In due time I shall transmit to the Congress such recommendations for changes in the present laws relating to these annual reports as appear to be pertinent and necessary.

Special consideration has been given by the commission to the annual reports relating to the financial transactions of the Government as a whole. In this connection the forms of the financial statements of the Government from early days to the present time have been examined. Further, in order that full information should be available, an investigation has been made of the forms of annual reports and budget statements, of the results of accounting, and of the terminology used by twenty or more foreign nations.

One of the consequences of this work is apparent in a modification of the form in which the gross receipts and disbursements of the

Government have been exhibited heretofore by the Secretary of the Treasury in his annual reports to the Congress.

These modifications are important as illustrations of what may be expected in improvement in the annual statements of the Government as a whole when final recommendations are made, based upon these extended studies. Further results of this work will be apparent when standard forms for financial reports of departments and establishments, which are now in preparation through cooperation with the responsible officials of various departments, are completed and published. It will then be evident how far short of realizable ideals have been our annual statements and reports of the past.

THE BUDGET

The United States is the only great Nation whose Government is operated without a budget. This fact seems to be more striking when it is considered that budgets and budget procedures are the outgrowth of democratic doctrines and have had an important part in the development of modern constitutional rights. The American Commonwealth has suffered much from irresponsibility on the part of its governing agencies. The constitutional purpose of a budget is to make government responsive to public opinion and responsible for its acts.

THE BUDGET AS AN ANNUAL PROGRAM

A budget should be the means for getting before the legislative branch, before the press, and before the people a definite annual program of business to be financed; it should be in the nature of a prospectus both of revenues and expenditures; it should comprehend every relation of the Government to the people, whether with reference to the rising of revenues or the rendering of service.

In many foreign countries the annual budget program is discussed with special reference to the revenue to be raised, the thought being that the raising of revenue bears more direct relation to welfare than does Government expenditure. Around questions of source of revenue political parties have been organized, and on such questions voters in the United States have taken sides since the first revenue law was proposed.

CITIZEN INTEREST IN EXPENDITURES

In political controversy it has been assumed generally that the individual citizen has little interest in what the Government spends. In my opinion, this has been a serious mistake, one which is becoming more serious each year. Now that population has become more dense, that large cities have developed, that people are required to live in congested centers, that the national resources frequently are the subject of private ownership and private control, and that transportation and other public-service facilities are held and operated by large corporations, what the Government does with nearly $1,000,000,000 each year is of as much concern to the average citizen as is the manner of obtaining this amount of money for public use. In the present inquiry special attention has been given to the expenditure side of the budget.

In prosecuting this inquiry, however, it has not been thought that arbitrary reductions should be made. The popular demand for economy has been to obtain the best service — the largest possible results for a given cost.

We want economy and efficiency; we want saving, and saving for a purpose. We want to save money to enable the Government to go into some of the beneficial projects which we are debarred from taking up now because we can not increase our expenditures. Projects affecting the public health, new public works, and other beneficial activities of government can be furthered if we are able to get a dollar of value for every dollar of the Government's money which we expend.

PUBLIC-WELFARE QUESTIONS

The principal governmental objects in which the people of the United States are interested include:

The national defense; the protection of persons and property; the promotion of friendly relations and the protection of American interests abroad; the regulation of commerce and industry; the promotion of agriculture, fisheries, forestry, and mining; the promotion of manufacturing, commerce, and banking; the promotion of transportation and communication; the postal service, including postal savings and parcel post; the care for and utilization of the public domain; the promotion of education, art, science, and recreation; the promotion of the public health; the care and education of the Indians and other wards of the Nation.

These are public-welfare questions in which I assume every citizen has a vital interest. I believe that every Member of Congress, as an official representative of the people, each editor, as a nonofficial representative of public opinion, each citizen, as a beneficiary of the trust imposed on officers of the Government, should be able readily to ascertain how much has been spent for each of these purposes; how much has been appropriated for the current year; how much the administration is asking for each of these purposes for the next fiscal year.

Furthermore, each person interested should have laid before him a clear, well-digested statement showing in detail whether moneys appropriated have been economically spent and whether each division or office has been efficiently run. This is the information which should be available each year in the form of a budget and in detail accounts and reports supporting the budget.

CONTINUANCE OF THE COMMISSION

I ask the continuance of this Commission on Economy and Efficiency because of the excellent beginning which has been made toward the reorganization of the machinery of this Government on business principles. I ask it because its work is entirely nonpartisan in character and ought to appeal to every citizen who wishes to give effectiveness to popular government, in which we feel a just pride. This work further commends itself for the reason that the cost of organization and work has been carefully considered at every point. Three months were taken in consideration of plans before the inquiry was begun; six months were then spent in preliminary investigations before the commission was organized; before March 3, 1911, when I asked for a continuation of the original appropriation for the current year, only $12,000 had been spent.

In organizing the commission my purpose was to obtain men eminently qualified for this character of work, and it may be said that it was found to be extremely difficult to find persons having such qualifications who would undertake the task. Several of the members of the commission were induced to take up the work as a personal sacrifice; in fact, considering the temporary character of the inquiry, it may be said that no member of the commission was moved by salary considerations. Only the public character of the work has made it possible for the Government to carry on such an inquiry except at a very much larger cost than has been incurred.

It is a matter of public record that the three largest insurance companies in New York, when under legislative investigation, spent more than $500,000 for expert services to assist the administration to put the business on a modern basis; but the economies the first year were more than tenfold the cost. I am informed that New York, Chicago, Boston, St. Louis, Cincinnati, Milwaukee, and other cities are prosecuting inquiries, the cost of which is largely disproportionate to the cost incurred by the Federal Government. Furthermore, these inquiries have the vigorous support and direct cooperation of citizen agencies which alone are spending not less than $200,000 per annum, and in several instances these combined agencies have been working not less than five years to put the cities on a business like basis, yet there is still much to be done.

The reason for bringing these facts to your attention is to suggest the magnitude of the task, the time necessary to its accomplishment, the professional skill which is essential to the successful handling of the work, the impossibility of carrying on such a work entirely with men who are at the same time engaged in the ordinary routine of administration. While in the nature of things the readjustment of organization and methods should continue indefinitely in order to adapt a great institution to the business in hand, ultimately this should be provided for as a part of the regular activities of some permanently organized agency. It is only after such a thorough inquiry has been made by experts who are not charged with the grinding details of official responsibility, however, that conclusions can be reached as to how this best can be done.

I sincerely hope that Congress will not, in its anxiety to reduce expenditures, economize by cutting off an appropriation which is likely to offer greater opportunity for real economy in the future than any other estimated for.

VIGOROUS PROSECUTION OF THE INQUIRY

Economies actually realized have more than justified the total expenditure of the inquiry to date, and the economies which will soon be made by Executive action, based upon the information now in hand, will be many times greater than those already realized. Furthermore, the inquiry is in process of establishing a sound basis for recommendations relating to changes in law which will be necessary in order to make effective the economies which can not be provided by Executive action alone. Still further, it should be realized that the progress made by the inquiry has been notable when measured against the magnitude of the task undertaken. The principal function of the inquiry has been that of coordination. The commission has acted and should continue to act as a central clearing house for the committees in the various departments and establishments. By no other means can the cooperation which is essential be developed and continued throughout the Government service.

Helpful as legislative investigations may be in obtaining information as a basis for legislative action, changes which affect technical operations and which have to do with the details of method and procedure, necessarily followed in effectively directing and controlling the activities of the various services, can be successfully accomplished only by highly trained experts, whose whole time shall be given to the work, acting in cooperation with those who are charged with the handling of administrative details. The upbuilding of efficient service must necessarily be an educational process. With each advance made there will remain to those who conduct the details of the business an additional incentive to increase the efficiency and to realize true economy in all branches of the Government service.

As has been said, the changes which have already been made are resulting in economies greater than the cost of the inquiry; reports in my hands, with recommendations, estimate approximately $2,000,-000 of possible annual economies; other subjects under investigation indicate much larger results. These represent only a few of the many services which should be subjected to a like painstaking inquiry. If this is done, it is beyond question that many millions of savings may be realized. Over and above the economy and increased efficiency which may be said to result from the work of the commission as such is an indirect result that can not well be measured. I refer to the influence which a vigorous, thoroughgoing executive inquiry has on each of the administrative units responsible to the Executive. The purpose being constructive, as soon as any subject is inquired into each of the services affected becomes at once alert to opportunities for improvement. So real is this that eagerness in many instances must be restrained. For example, when reports were requested on the subject of handling and filing correspondence, so many changes were begun that it became necessary to issue a letter to heads of departments requesting them not to permit further changes until the results had been reported and uniform plans of action had been agreed upon. To have permitted each of the hundred of offices to undertake changes on their own initiative would merely have added to the confusion.

Much time and expense are necessary to get an inquiry of this kind started, to lay the foundation for sound judgment, and to develop the momentum required to accomplish definite results. This initial work has been done. The inquiry with its constructive measures is well under way. The work should now be prosecuted with vigor and receive the financial support necessary to make it most effective during the next fiscal year.

In this relation it may be said that the expenditure for the inquiry during the present fiscal year is at the rate of $130,000. The mass of information which must be collected, digested, and summarized pertaining to each subject of inquiry is enormous. From the results obtained it is evident that every dollar which is spent in the prosecution of the inquiry in the future will result in manifold savings. Every economy which has been or will be effected through changes in organization or method will inure to the benefit of the Government and of the people in increasing measure through the years which follow. It is clearly the part of wisdom to provide for the coming year means at least equal to those available during the current year, and in my opinion the appropriation should be increased to $200,000 and an additional amount of $50,000 should be provided for the publication of those results which will be of continuing value to officers of the Government and to the people.

WM. H. TAFT

BIBLIOGRAPHICAL AIDS

Asterioks after titles refer to books currently available in paperback editions.

SOURCE MATERIALS

The primary source for the study of William Howard Taft is his collection of papers at the Library of Congress, consisting of nearly a half-million documents covering every period of his life. Taft's decisions as superior court judge of Ohio appear in The Weekly Law Bulletin and Ohio Law Journal of 1887-90. Taft himself did not write a great deal; in addition to published works listed below, he wrote essays on Popular Government, Its Essence, Its Performance and its Perils (1913) and The Anti-Trust Act and the Supreme Court (1914).

Israel, Fred, ed. State of the Union Messages of the Presidents. 3 vols. New York: Chelsea House, 1966. Contains an introduction by Arthur Schlesinger that discusses major themes of the messages and a 79-page index. The messages are presented without interpretation.

Richardson, James D., ed. Messages and Papers of the Presidents. Vols. XVI and XVII. Washington: Bureau of National Literature, 1912.

Taft, William Howard. Ethics in Service. New Haven: Yale University Press, 1915. Yale Lecture Series.

Taft, William Howard. Our Chief Magistrate and His Powers. New York: Columbia University Press, 1916. A lecture series at Columbia.

Taft, William Howard. The President and His Powers. New York: Columbia University Press, 1916.

Taft, William Howard. The Presidency, Its Duties, Its Powers, Its Opportunities and Limitations. New York: C. Scribners Sons, 1916. A series of three lectures given by Taft at the University of Virginia.

BIOGRAPHIES

Pringle, Henry Fowles. The Life and Times of William Howard Taft. 2 vols. New York: Farrar and Rinehart, 1939. The definitive biography of Taft, drawing heavily on material in the Library of Congress. It contains an exhaustive bibliography.

Ross, Ishbel. An American Family; The Tafts, 1678 to 1964. Cleveland: World Publishing Co., 1964. An interesting and comprehensive account of a great family, in which William Howard Taft plays a central part.

ESSAYS

Competent essays on William Howard Taft appear in most of the major encyclopedias. The article in the Encyclopedia Britannica is written by George W. Wickersham, Taft's attorney general. The bibliography is unsatisfactory, however. Henry F. Pringle's article in the Encyclopedia Americana is comprehensive but contains no bibliography. George Mowry is the author of the Collier's Encyclopedia article, and a rather extensive treatment by John M. Blum appears in The World Book Encyclopedia. Finally, Pringle is the author of the essay in the Dictionary of American Biography. Additional essays and articles can be found by consulting the Reader's Guide to Periodical Literature and the Social Sciences and Humanities Index. Following is a selection of recommended articles:

Campbell, J. P. "Taft, Roosevelt and the Arbitration Treaties of 1911," Journal of American History, LIII (September, 1966).

Danelski, D.J. "Supreme Court Justice Steps Down," Yale Review, LIV (March, 1965), 411-25.

Hahn, H. "President Taft and the Discipline of Patronage," Journal of Politics, XVIII (May, 1966), 368-90.

Hess, Stephen. "Big Bill Taft," American Heritage, XVII (October, 1966), 32-7.

Jeffries, Ona Griffin. "Four Years of Strife: William Howard Taft and Helen Taft," in her In and Out of the White House. New York, 1960.

Kutler, S.I. "Chief Justice Taft, National Regulation and the Commerce Power," Journal of American History, LI (March, 1965), 56-68.

Marx, Rudolf. "Taft" in his Health of the Presidents. New York:
Putnam, 1960.

Seltzer, Louis B. "Episode in a Railroad Station," Colliers, CXXXVII
(September 14, 1956), 56-7.

Smith, Bessie White. "Taft" in her Romances of the Presidents. Boston: Lothrop, Lee and Shepard, 1932.

Whytlaw, M.G. "O, Mr. President," Parents Magazine, XXIII (November, 1948), 68.

MONOGRAPHS AND SPECIAL AREAS

Butt, Archibald W. Taft and Roosevelt: The Intimate Letters of
Archie Butt. Garden City: Doubleday, Doran & Co., 1930.

Hess, Stephen. America's Political Dynasties; from Adams to Kennedy.
New York: Doubleday, 1966. Discusses sixteen political families
including the Tafts.

Kelly, Frank K. The Fight for the White House; The Story of 1912.
New York: Thomas Y. Crowell, 1961. A month by month account
of the struggle the three candidates waged for the presidency.

Manners, William. TR & Will; A Friendship That Split the Republican
Party. New York: Harcourt, Brace & World, 1969. A professionally
written account of the dramatic events of 1908-1919. Contains an
excellent bibliography.

Odegard, Peter H. Religion and Politics. Dobbs Ferry, N.Y.: Oceana,
1960.

Umbreit, Kenneth Bernard. Our Eleven Chief Justices: A History of
the Supreme Court in Terms of Their Personalities. New York:
Harper & Brothers, 1938.

THE PROGRESSIVE ERA

Abrams, Richard M. ed. Issues of the Populist and Progressive
Period. New York: Harper & Bros., 1969.

Forcey, Charles. The Crossroads of Liberalism. New York: Oxford,
1961.*

Hofstadter, Richard. The Age of Reform; from Bryan to F.D.R. New York: Alfred Knopf, 1955.* An analysis of the primary movements of reform from 1890 to the first world war.

Hofstadter, Richard, ed. The Progressive Movement, 1900-1915. New York: Prentice Hall, 1964.* An enlightening background study of the period.

Mann, A. The Progressive Era. New York: Holt, Rhinehart & Winston, 1963.

Mowry, George E. Theodore Roosevelt and The Progressive Movement. New York: Hill & Wang, 1946.* Treats the movement from 1909 to 1919, including the Republican and Bull Moose conventions of 1912.

Nye, Russell B. Midwestern Progressive Politics. East Lansing: Michigan State University Press, 1951.* Traces rise and fall of Progressivism from days of the Grangers through Bryan and LaFollette.

Pinchot, Gifford. Breaking New Ground. New York: Harcourt, Brace, 1947. Autobiography stressing years 1889 to 1912 and the new emphasis on conservation.

Warner, Hoyt L. Progressivism in Ohio, 1897-1917. Columbus: Ohio State University Press, 1965. Comprehensive study of local history of reform in Ohio.

Wiebe, Robert H. Businessmen and Reform: A Study of the Progressive Movement. Cambridge: Harvard University Press, 1962.

Wilensky, Norman M. Conservatives in the Progressive Era. Gainsville: University of Florida, 1965.*

THE PRESIDENCY

American Heritage. ed. History of the American Presidency. New York: American Heritage, 1968.

Bailey, Thomas A. Presidential Greatness: The Image and Man from George Washington to the Present. New York: Appleton, 1966.* Critical and subjective, arranged topically rather than chronologically. Excellent bibliography.

Burns, James MacGregor. Presidential Government — The Crucible of Leadership. Boston: Houghton Mifflin, 1966.* The relationship of the President to Congress is the theme of this excellent study.

Cable, Mary. Avenue of the Presidents. Boston: Houghton Mifflin, 1969.

Corwin, Edward S. The President: Offices and Powers. New York: New York University Press, 1957.*

Filler, Louis, ed. The President Speaks: From McKinley to Lyndon Johnson. New York: G.P. Putnam's Sons, 1966.*

Kane, Joseph Nathan. Facts About the Presidents. New York: H.W. Wilson, 1959. Comparative and biographical data.

Koenig, Louis W. The Chief Executive. New York: Harcourt, Brace & World, 1964. Authoritative study of presidential powers.

Laski, Harold. The American Presidency. New York: Grosset and Dunlop, 1958.

Lorant, Stefan. Glorious Burden: The American Presidency. New York: Harper and Row, 1969. An enlargement and updated version of The Presidency: A Pictoral History of Presidential Elections, 1951.

Neustadt, Richard E. Presidential Power — The Politics of Leadership. New York: John Wiley & Sons, 1960.*

Rossiter, Clinton. The American Presidency. New York: Harcourt, Brace, 1956.* Shows how the powers of the Presidency have steadily gained over the limitations.

Schlesinger, Arthur M. and Israel, Fred L. eds. A History of Presidential Elections, 1789-1968. 4 vols. New York: Chelsea House, forthcoming.

Tugwell, Rexford G. The Enlargement of the Presidency. Garden City: Doubleday, 1960. An account of the growth of the office.

Warren, Sidney. The President as World Leader. Philadelphia: J.B. Lippincott, 1964.* Assessment of United States presidents' assumption of global responsibilities, from Theodore Roosevelt through John Kennedy.

Whitney, David C. Graphic Story of the American Presidents. New York: Doubleday, 1968.

Wildansky, Aaron. The Presidency. Boston: Little Brown, 1969.

NAME INDEX

TITLES IN THE OCEANA
PRESIDENTIAL CHRONOLOGY SERIES
Reference books containing
Chronology—Documents—Bibliographical Aids
for each President covered.
Series Editor: **Howard F. Bremer**

GEORGE WASHINGTON*
edited by Howard F. Bremer

JOHN ADAMS*
edited by Howard F. Bremer

JAMES BUCHANAN*
edited by Irving J. Sloan

GROVER CLEVELAND**
edited by Robert I. Vexler

FRANKLIN PIERCE*
edited by Irving J. Sloan

ULYSSES S. GRANT**
edited by Philip R. Moran

MARTIN VAN BUREN**
edited by Irving J. Sloan

THEODORE ROOSEVELT**
edited by Gilbert Black

BENJAMIN HARRISON*
edited by Harry J. Sievers

JAMES MONROE*
edited by Ian Elliot

WOODROW WILSON**
edited by Robert I. Vexler

RUTHERFORD B. HAYES*
edited by Arthur Bishop

ANDREW JACKSON**
edited by Ronald Shaw

JAMES MADISON**
edited by Ian Elliot

HARRY S TRUMAN***
edited by Howard B. Furer

WARREN HARDING**
edited by Philip Moran

DWIGHT D. EISENHOWER***
edited by Robert I. Vexler

JAMES K. POLK*
edited by John J. Farrell

JOHN QUINCY ADAMS*
edited by Kenneth Jones

HARRISON/TYLER***
edited by David A. Durfee

ABRAHAM LINCOLN***
edited by Ian Elliot

GARFIELD/ARTHUR***
edited by Howard B. Furer

WILLIAM McKINLEY
edited by Harry J. Sievers

ANDREW JOHNSON
edited by John N. Dickinson

WILLIAM HOWARD TAFT
edited by Gilbert Black

CALVIN COOLIDGE
edited by Philip Moran

Available Soon

JOHN F. KENNEDY
edited by Ralph A. Stone

THOMAS JEFFERSON
edited by Arthur Bishop

TAYLOR/FILLMORE
edited by John J. Farrell

LYNDON B. JOHNSON
edited by Howard B. Furer

FRANKLIN D. ROOSEVELT
edited by Howard F. Bremer

HERBERT HOOVER
edited by Arnold Rice

*   96 pages, $3.00/B
** 128 pages, $4.00/B
*** 160 pages, $5.00/B